PENGUIN BOOKS

# WHO KILLED FREDDIE MILLS?

Tony Van den Bergh was educated in misery at Repton School, and afterwards trained at RADA. He began writing for radio immediately after World War II and is the author of more than 1,000 radio plays and documentaries, including *The Ruth Ellis Story*, *Jack the Ripper*, *The A6 Murder* (with Alan Burgess) and *Dead on Arrival*. His varied journalistic career includes work for the *Sunday Times* as journalist on the run with the South London gang leader Charlie Richardson, when Richardson escaped from prison.

Tony Van den Bergh has presented medical programmes for both radio and television, and received a World Special Award in 1988 for *Treat Me Gently*, in which, under spinal anaesthetic, he gave a running commentary as he underwent a hip-replacement operation. Himself once an amateur boxer, he has been an inspector for the British Boxing Board of Control, and a boxing commentator for both ITV and BBC radio and television.

He was also co-founder and managing director of Four Square Books and is the author of six books including *The Jack Johnson Story*, *The Padded Ring* and (with Laurence Marks) *Diminished Responsibility*. He lives in Hampstead, London.

G000243154

TONY VAN DEN BERGH

WHO KILLED FREDDIE MILLS?

PENGUIN BOOKS

PENGUIN BOOKS

Published by the Penguin Group
Penguin Books Ltd, 27 Wrights Lane, London W8 5TZ, England
Penguin Books USA Inc., 375 Hudson Street, New York, New York 10014, USA
Penguin Books Australia Ltd, Ringwood, Victoria, Australia
Penguin Books Canada Ltd, 10 Alcorn Avenue, Toronto, Ontario, Canada M4V 3B2
Penguin Books (NZ) Ltd, 182–190 Wairau Road, Auckland 10, New Zealand

Penguin Books Ltd, Registered Offices: Harmondsworth, Middlesex, England

First published by Constable & Co. Ltd 1991
Published in Penguin Books 1993
1 3 5 7 9 10 8 6 4 2

Printed in England by Clays Ltd, St Ives plc

TO CAPTAIN JACKIE HOPWOOD,
BOXER, MATCH-MAKER,
MANAGER AND TRUE FRIEND
FOR MORE THAN FIFTY YEARS.

Death is a maiden
Raven-haired and secretive.
Clad in heavy garments
Yet naked and slovenly to the human eye.
Always taking,
Giving no known return.

# ILLUSTRATIONS

# ACKNOWLEDGEMENTS

This research has covered many years, with the result that some of those who helped me with my initial inquiries are now dead. This doesn't lessen my gratitude to them and to all those who have actively helped me, made suggestions, or raised lines of inquiry to be followed. In particular I am indebted to: Manuel Abrew; Jarvis Astair; Bill Bavin; Peter Barry; Professor J.A.N. Corsellis, FRCP, F.R.C.Path, F.R.C.Psy; Mickey Duff; Dr Helen Grant, MD, FRCP; Dr Peter Harvey, MA, MB, B.Chir, FRCP; Captain Jackie Hopwood; Derek Horne; Dr Desmond Kelly, MD, FRCP, F.R.C.Psy, DPM; Charles Kray; Chrissie Mills; Ron Oliver; Charles Richardson; Commander Nipper Read; Dr William Sargant, MA, MB, B.Chir, FRCP, F.R.C.Psy; Professor Cedric Keith Simpson, CBE, MD, FRCP, F.R.C.Path, LL D; Annette Spence, RGN, Dip Psy, Dip Human Sexuality; Peta Steel; Alec Steen; Dr Anthony Storr, MB, B.Chir, FRCP, F.R.C.Psy; and Ruth White.

T.V.d.B.
1991

# PROLOGUE

I met Freddie Mills for the first time on 20 June 1942, the night he took the lightheavyweight championship from Len Harvey by knocking out the master-boxer in the second round. Harvey was punched through the ropes and failed to get back in time to beat the count.

I was a friend of Harvey and so, illogically, felt a certain animosity towards his young conqueror. Boxing is a brutal, emotional sport. Most of the audience get their kicks by identifying with one of the boxers. This allows puny little men to imagine they are giants and cowards to feel they're heroes.

Len Harvey, the Plymouth-born boxer, had fought at every weight from fly to heavy and, up to that evening, had never been KO'd. But he'd been out of serious boxing for the four years of war and as an officer in the RAF hadn't had the time or the inclination – as he told me when acting as my inter-round expert during the boxing commentary I gave on the first night of commercial television – for the commitment to training that this savage industry demands.

As a boxing writer I suspected that Harvey had accepted the contest solely for the purse, and hadn't trained as conscientiously as he would have done in pre-war days. A four-year break from serious boxing causes ring-rust; timing deteriorates and the reflexes slow. Nevertheless I had hoped Harvey would be the exception and would defy the passing of the years.

In stark comparison to the graceful, classic boxing of Len Harvey, Mills seemed brash and unskilful, relying on sheer strength, youth and aggression. It was the classic encounter of boxer versus puncher. This time the puncher won.

My rather ridiculous initial antipathy to the new champion for beating my friend lasted only until I went into his dressing-room to congratulate him. Freddie was sitting on the massage bench, his head swathed in a towel, as Nat Seller, his trainer, cut the bandages and plaster from his fists. Freddie was behaving just like a small boy who'd been given the largest ice-cream in the world. His eyes were darting from side to side as he thanked everyone in sight for their support. He bubbled with excitement and clearly wasn't yet able to believe he was the new champion. Nat Seller was having difficulty not cutting Freddie's fingers, since the boxer wanted to shake hands with everyone.

Over the following years, as an inspector of the British Boxing Board of Control and then boxing commentator for BBC radio and TV, I was frequently in Mills's company. I officiated as inspector for both of his world championship contests against the likeable American Gus Lesnevich, consoling him after he was knocked out in their first meeting and congratulating him when he took the crown in their return match.

I became a friend . . . but then Mills had hundreds of friends. He loved people. I never became really close to him.

After Freddie retired from the ring, I still met him frequently at charity tournaments and in radio and television studios. Whilst he was always a popular guest on celebrity shows, I was building a modest name for myself as a panellist. On radio I took over from Richard Dimbleby in *Twenty Questions* under the chairmanship of that much maligned but generous man, Gilbert Harding. I was also performing weekly on the long-running *The Name's the Same*, as well as acting as champion for men's opinions in *How to Manage Men* against the formidable Fanny Cradock. I also substituted for Dimbleby in *What's My Line* and was a full-time panellist in the programme on BBC TV, *Table Talk*.

One of my fellow panellists on *The Name's the Same* was that fascinating, elfin, platinum blond American, Frances Day. Frances, a star of musical comedy, recalls memories even today – of yards and yards of floating tulle and lilting songs. When Frances suggested that Freddie and I should join her in a cabaret act I was both flattered and delighted. As far as Freddie was concerned it meant a new audience and for him that was all-important.

The scenario for our act was a series of short and witty exchanges between the traditional dumb blonde, the macho numbskull and the aesthetic, out-of-this-world egghead. I was cast as the high-brow, which amused and amazed me for I've always been justly modest about my intellectual capacity. We concluded our act with Freddie and me singing the single word 'It's' and Frances supplying the 'D'lightful, d'licious, d'lovely'.

When I read the headlines 'Freddie Mills dead', 'Freddie Mills shot', 'Freddie Mills – MURDER!', I was naturally enormously shocked and sad. When, later, I learned that the coroner's verdict was suicide, I reacted angrily. I could not envisage any circumstances which would cause the brave, ebullient, outgoing Freddie Mills I knew to take his own life. Freddie had everything an ordinary man could want . . . and Freddie had always appeared the most normal of humans. He had a worshipping wife, Chrissie, two young girls he clearly adored and never tired of talking about, and a comfortable home, Joggi Villa, on Denmark Hill. Furthermore he was still an immensely popular character in the British social and theatrical scene and relished the hero-worship which was accorded him everywhere he went.

Today I still reject the suicide verdict though my opinion is not so firmly based as it was at the time. Over the years, as a medical journalist and playwright, I have learned, from leading psychologists and psychiatrists writing about the urges some of us have for self-destruction, that it is possible for the most apparently gregarious of people to have shadowy corners in the mind which are unsuspected even by those closest to them.

At the time my rejection of the suicide verdict was so strong that I wasn't content to air my views whenever possible, as did many of Freddie's boxing colleagues and friends, but set out to investigate what had happened.

As Shakespeare wrote: 'Rumour is a pipe Blown by surmises, jealousies, conjectures . . .' And in the months following Freddie Mills's death, the pipe never ceased being blown. Everyone, however remotely connected with boxing and London night-life, had his own pet theory. Everyone had inside information.

Teddy Waltham, former professional welterweight, referee and, at the time, general secretary of the British Boxing Board of Control, was one of the first to air his view that Freddie had been murdered. Another early proponent of this theory was the tsar of British boxing, 'Jovial' Jack Solomons, the ex-fishmonger. He told me: 'Tony, I knew Freddie as well as anybody. Freddie commit suicide . . . you must be joking!' Both refused to accept the coroner's verdict.

As the months passed it might have been expected that the rumours would evaporate as subsequent events proved them to be without substance. But the rumours didn't abate. Far from it. In the changing rooms at gymnasiums and in the Soho back alleys, in the club bars and snooker-rooms, even wilder theories surfaced.

If the coroner were correct and Mills *had* killed himself, what could have been the reasons for the ex-champion taking his own life? Every know-all had inside information. 'Of course, very few people knew that Freddie . . .' Then the tongues wagged and imaginations were let loose.

There were as many rumours, however, as to who might have killed Mills, and why, as there were about his suicide. Again, know-alls hinted to anyone who'd listen that they were among the tiny circle who actually knew the truth. 'Now, don't tell anyone else, for God's sake, but actually . . .' Each rumour was said to have come from an impeccable source.

I traced these rumours as well as I could, first for a radio documentary for Radio 4 and then for a series of articles. The more I searched, the more involved the mystery became. Eventually I decided to write a book about it.

I paid several visits to Joggi Villa to talk to, and record, Chrissie Mills. I also chatted to friends of the family and members of the boxing fraternity, who all had their own views about his death. I recorded those of Teddy Waltham and Jack Solomons; I lunched with Bill Bavin, a close friend of Mills, who had advised him about buying property and investing the thousands his fists had earned him in the ring and who, in his own book on Mills's death, *The Strange Death of Freddie Mills* (Howard Baker Press Ltd, 1975), had suggested the involvement of the Richardson gang.

I was impressed with the certainty with which each of these said that Freddie Mills must have been murdered. 'Suicide? Not Freddie!'

Before putting the final full-stop to my book I went to interview Commander 'Nipper' Read of Scotland Yard, who had reopened the case in 1961. By then I'd begun to accept the theory that the notorious Kray twins had been responsible. But Read said he hadn't found any evidence to sustain such an accusation, and in view of his certainty I felt my book was heading nowhere. Reluctantly I abandoned the project.

Meanwhile, with Laurence Marks, co-author of the popular TV series *Shine on Harvey Moon* and *The New Statesman*, and now one of our most successful scriptwriters, I had written *Diminished Responsibility*, the story of the tragic life and death of club-hostess Ruth Ellis. In almost every other civilized Western society, Ruth Ellis would have served only a nominal sentence. In Italy, a woman found guilty of an almost identical murder was sentenced to two years . . . suspended. They looked upon it as a *crime passionnel*. But at the time the British Establishment was determined to retain capital punishment and at the direction of an appalling Home Secretary Ruth Ellis was hanged.

When, in 1990, Penguin bought the paperback rights of *Diminished Responsibility*, I discussed with them the possibility of my writing another book for their 'True Crime' series. They invited my suggestions and I proposed either the case of Frederick Gordon Cummings, a mass-murderer of prostitutes in the black-out of wartime London (a story I'd dramatized for BBC Radio 4 under the title *Just Like Leslie Howard*) or *Who Killed Freddie Mills?*

While we were still discussing the matter I wrote to the Westminster coroner asking if I might read the records of the inquest, the coroner's notes and the report of the Home Office pathologist. This had been refused during my previous research. Since then the coroner concerned had died and his successor generously gave his permission.

In the Westminster Coroner's Court – an almost country-cottage-like building quite out of character for so macabre a centre – I read exactly what evidence had been given in court by members of the staff at Mills's night-club, who had gone out to try and awaken their employer as he sat, dead, in the back seat of his car. I also read the evidence given by the police on the spot and by Andy Ho, Mills's Chinese partner who, extraordinarily, never went out to the yard himself, even when the doorman and head-waiter reported that they could not waken Mills.

I was surprised at the certainty with which the coroner had reached a verdict of suicide, for it seemed to me there were several unexplained discrepancies in the evidence. In fact, there were too many unanswered questions. I knew then why I must write this book, and my publishers agreed with me.

So I started my research all over again. This time I had new rumours to investigate, new people to see. I talked to Charles Kray, who is now rebuilding his life after a ten-year sentence and is somewhat at odds with the twin brothers over the film made about their lives. I talked to my close friend Charles Richardson, who firmly believes Mills killed himself. I talked to ex-boxers, his sparring-partners and opponents, and with actors and actresses who had become his friends after he had hung up his gloves. I listened to men from the twilight world of crime, and to the Hammersmith police.

And, most interesting of all, I finally became aware of a Soho Chinese connection.

# 1

SATURDAY 24 July 1965 was an unusually cold day for midsummer. The wind was biting, but it was dry and bright.

Over the years most families develop a weekend routine and the Mills family was no exception. However, their routine was partly determined by the fact that Saturday was a working day as far as the head of the family was concerned. Shortly after ten on Saturday evenings Mills would kiss his wife and daughters goodbye before driving his silver-grey Citroën to the Freddie Mills Nite Spot in Goslett Yard, Soho.

He would reach Soho about half-past ten, and, having parked and locked his car, would go into the club, check the evening's bookings with his partner, Andy Ho, inspect the kitchen, taste the food in preparation, and ensure that everything was clean. He would always take time to chat with his staff and find out if any problems had arisen since the previous evening. Then he would change his jacket and get himself ready to glad-hand the guests.

The Mills home on Denmark Hill in South London was a typical family house in a middle-class area. Freddie and Chrissie had named it 'Joggi Villa'. As a child, Chrissie had been unable to pronounce the word 'dog', saying 'jog' instead, and 'Jog' was also Freddie's pet name for his wife.

Joggi Villa had a small, narrow hall leading from the front door into the lounge and to the bottom of the stairs. Beyond the lounge were the doors into the dining-room and kitchen. The lounge windows opened on to the main road, whilst those of the kitchen and dining-room looked over the back garden and the small swimming-pool Mills had built for his two young daughters. Off the dining-room was a study where, after her husband's death, Chrissie kept mementoes of Freddie's boxing career: silver cups, illuminated addresses, photographs, cartoons, programmes, newspaper cuttings, the framed Freedom of the City of Bournemouth and, in pride of place, a life-size model of the champion in fighting stance.

Although both the front and back gardens were small, Mills enjoyed playing the gardener. He preferred working in the swimming-pool area at the back because there he had the better chance of being able to work in peace. Whenever he cut the grass or pruned the roses in the front garden, passers-by would recognize him, stop for a chat, and inevitably, would describe to him how they had cheered him on during his fights. Freddie never ignored well-wishers, whether friends, acquaintances or total strangers. He was always ready to drop whatever he was doing to answer questions, talk about his ring battles and his opinion of the merits of the current batch of fighters. A few seconds would spin out into minutes and the lawn would remain unmown and the flowerbeds untrimmed. It was a family joke that when Freddie worked in the front garden, he'd take an hour or more to do five minutes' real work.

On this particular Saturday, he'd got up early. Chrissie had been complaining that the hydrangeas in the centre of the front lawn were untidy.

'They look a little sad,' she'd told him. 'Why don't you cut them back?'

Mills had recently suffered from a mild attack of pneumonia, so he wrapped himself up warmly before he started work with his secateurs. Then he swept up the cuttings ready to be burned. Noticing that the curtains of their bedroom were drawn back, he concluded that Chrissie was up, and called to her: 'Look, Mummy. Doesn't it all look lovely now?'

To anyone eavesdropping it must have sounded a little incongruous to hear a broken-nosed, cauliflower-eared, ex-boxer calling his wife 'Mummy'. He never used this expression outside Joggi Villa, and would have been embarrassed if any outsider had heard him because it would have spoiled the macho image which was so important to him. Supermen don't use such endearments.

Chrissie Mills looked down from the bedroom window. Her husband's enthusiasm was always infectious.

'Yes, it's fine, wonderful.' Then, after a short pause, she added: 'Now, what about the grass? That needs doing too, you know.'

Freddie raised his hands above his head as if surrendering to an opponent. 'Gee, you're a slave-driver.' Then he laughed and went to the garden shed to collect the lawn-mower.

This good-humour and his readiness to tidy up the garden would surely have been strange reactions in a man who had decided to take his own life. He would have been pottering about carrying out small jobs knowing that within sixteen hours his body would be lying cold on a morgue slab!

By the time Doris Budgeon, a close friend of Chrissie, had looked in for her usual Saturday morning cup of tea, the lawn was trim and the mower back in the shed. On Saturday nights Chrissie would join her husband for a late supper at his club, usually around midnight. Before leaving Joggi Villa she would hand over the care of Susan and Amanda, their daughters, to Doris Budgeon, and in case she would be in a hurry in the evening and forget to give Doris all her instructions, she'd always invite her friend to call in early for a few minutes during the morning. Apart from discussing the two children, they both enjoyed a social chat.

After breakfast on this particular morning, the whole family went out to do the week's shopping. They took both their cars – Freddie's Citroën and Chrissie's Mini – so that Chrissie and the children could come straight home after paying the bill. Invariably Freddie would be held up in the supermarket, playing and horsing about with children. Freddie was always a Pied Piper.

Recalling that morning, Chrissie told me: 'Freddie showed not the slightest sign that he was worried by anything. It was a really happy day: a good day. Freddie was in one of his best moods and seemed as if he hadn't a care in the world. We all enjoyed ourselves.'

It was close to lunch-time when Freddie finally shed his young followers and followed his family home. After eating, Freddie and Chrissie chatted as they washed up. Then having gone out for twenty minutes to buy cigarettes, Freddie went upstairs to bed while the children got on with their homework. Freddie's wasn't the routine of the tired businessman, but a necessary preparation for a full night's work.

Chrissie didn't wake him until just before eight in the evening. After washing and dressing, Freddie went down to the kitchen to watch his daughters give a dancing display they'd devised specially for him. With his love of showbiz, Freddie always encouraged Susan and Mandy to sing, dance and act. He relaxed in an easy chair brought in from the lounge. Both his daughters were in their night-gowns so they could go straight to bed after they'd made their final curtseys: that at least was the theory. He ate a light supper of haddock with a poached egg on top; he would have a heavier meal early on Sunday morning at the club with Chrissie. While he ate, the usual argument took place between his daughters and their mother, the children appealing to be allowed to stay up 'just a little longer' to watch the Morecambe and Wise show on television.

Chrissie said: 'No! You've already been allowed to stay up late to entertain your Dad.'

When the girls turned to their father, Freddie, more indulgent than his wife, gave way, arguing with Chrissie that as the next day was Sunday they could lie in late to make up for any loss of sleep. A daughter on either knee, he watched the double act on the box before putting on a Beatles' record and dancing the Twist with Mandy. Then he carried them both up to bed. The time of the transmission of the Morecambe and Wise show confirms Chrissie's estimate that Mills couldn't possibly have left Joggi Villa until well after ten o'clock that night. He still showed no signs of worry or stress.

By the time he was ready to leave, Doris Budgeon had arrived, and Mills suggested that Chrissie might like to accompany him to the club there and then, instead of joining him later as usual. If Chrissie had agreed to this, she would surely have foiled any plans to kill himself alone in his car: therefore his invitation to her was strange if, indeed, he had decided to commit suicide.

From the bedroom where she was putting the children to sleep, Chrissie called down to him: 'I'd like to come, but if I come with you in the Citroën, I shan't be able to drive back here because Donny's borrowed the Mini. I'll have to wait till he gets back with it or I'll be stuck at the club.'

Donny was Chrissie's son by her first marriage to Don McCorkindale, the former South African heavyweight champion who'd also been managed by her father.

When Chrissie made up her mind there was no use arguing, so Freddie Mills, having kissed her goodnight, went out to the garage and drove off in the Citroën.

That was the last time Chrissie saw her husband alive.

Donny and his wife didn't get back from their party until after twelve. Chrissie wasn't pleased with her son for breaking his word. She is a woman who flares up quickly and speaks her mind, but afterwards is prepared to put any unpleasantness behind her. Having told Donny that his thoughtlessness had prevented her joining Freddie earlier, she smiled to show that her anger had burned out and said: 'As you're so late, you might as well both come with me to the club. You could probably do with something to eat by now.'

The exact time they left Denmark Hill cannot be established for certain, but Chrissie believes it must have been between after twelve and twelve-thirty.

They arrived at the club's front door in Charing Cross Road some time between twelve forty-five and one-fifteen. As she climbed out of the Mini, Chrissie Mills sniffed the night air. It was chilly for July and she wondered if her husband had had the sense to wrap up warmly when he'd gone out for his usual late-night nap in his car. She'd had to nurse him through his pneumonia and knew that he wasn't nearly as tough as he always pretended.

Andy Ho, her husband's partner, had evidently been waiting for her. Coming across the pavement he held her car door open. 'I've been trying to ring you . . .' (Later she learnt that he had telephoned after she left and had left an urgent message with Mrs Budgeon for her to ring him.)

Chrissie ignored him, brushing his arm away from her. She didn't like Ho and had told him so to his face. They seldom agreed on anything and two days previously they had had a bitter disagreement over the phone. Ho had hung up on her, which Chrissie had considered unforgivably rude. She had told Freddie that she wished he would be more selective of those friends he would have to work with, and had pointed out that, in her view, Ho contributed nothing to the partnership: people joined the club because of Freddie.

Ho persisted, putting his hand on her arm. Chrissie turned her back on him, and led the way towards the club.

Afterwards, she said: 'Nothing daunted, he grabbed my shoulder and told me: "Chrissie, you *must* come round the corner." I said: "Look here, Andy. Leave me alone. I don't want anything to do with you."'

'He said: "You've just *got* to come round to the car. Freddie's asleep in the back and we can't wake him." By this time he'd managed to propel me half-way down Goslett Yard. When I got there, I saw Freddie was sitting in the back of the car behind the front passenger seat. The window by him was right down; wide open. So I went round the car to the other side, opened the rear door and got in behind the driver's seat.'

Sitting in the car beside her husband, Chrissie put her arm about his shoulder. He felt stiff and cold. Even then she didn't suspect the truth.

'I thought to myself: "Oh, God, sitting here with the bloody window wide open after suffering from pneumonia! It's mad!" So I moved closer to him to give him my warmth. But I couldn't get really close because there was something hard and cold between us . . . between his right leg and my left . . . something metal. I couldn't see Freddie's face properly because the only light came from an old lamp on the yard wall.'

Still believing her husband had been taken ill, Mrs Mills tried to draw him closer to her. His head lolled sideways against her shoulder.

'I thought, "I'll get nearer still. I'll move whatever this is between us!" I thought it might be the starting-handle of the car; Freddie always seemed to be leaving it on the back seat. So I pushed him a little away from me to give me room. As I did so, I saw that my white costume was covered in something wet and red. I thought: "Oh, my God!"'

Years later Chrissie Mills could remember every detail of that terrible scene as though it had been filmed in her mind in slow motion.

'I pulled myself together. I thought that perhaps Freddie had fallen sideways and cut his mouth on that starting-handle. I thought: "He's dozed off and hit his mouth on it." By this time I'd got my left arm free, and I took what I assumed to be the starting-handle and just slewed it across my legs and propped it against the right-hand rear door. Then I began to turn to put my arms around Freddie again. As I did so the penny dropped. It *wasn't* the starting-handle, it was a gun! Donny, my son, was standing outside the car watching me. I screamed to him: "It's a gun, Donny! Phone the police! An ambulance . . . a doctor . . . it's very bad. Oh, my God!"'

When he heard his mother scream, Donny McCorkindale snatched open the car door and grabbed her by her arms. Then, with the help of his wife, he half-carried Chrissie out of the car and across the few yards to the club's rear entrance. By now Chrissie was totally distraught and between screams and sobs was beseeching the club staff to pray for Freddie's soul. She fell into a chair, burying her head in her arms.

Only now did Andy Ho telephone for an ambulance. There are different versions of the times involved, so it is now impossible to say accurately how long the delay had been.

Within five minutes the ambulance arrived and rushed Freddie Mills to the Casualty Department of the Middlesex Hospital in Mortimer Street. He was entered in their register as DOA, Dead on Arrival.

The hospital telephoned the police. This was the first intimation the police had of Mills's death.

By the time the police arrived at the club – and there are varying estimates of just when that was – Donny had driven his mother away from the tragic scene. By then, although they hadn't heard from the hospital, Donny had accepted that his father-in-law was dead. Having persuaded Chrissie to drink a large brandy in the club, he tried to get her to agree to go home as there was nothing to be done, pointing out that the club guests had realized that something terrible had happened, and suggesting that 'her Freddie', as club proprietor, would have wanted her to conceal the truth from them as long possible.

Chrissie told me that she had felt as though nothing was real and she was living through some terrible nightmare. Eventually she agreed to leave the club, but she couldn't yet go home and face their children. She asked Donny to telephone her friends Pat and Joe: Pat was better known to the public as Ann Shelton, the singing star. Ann and her husband were Catholics and Chrissie needed the support of friends of her faith.

By the time Donny had driven his mother to her friends' flat, Ann Shelton had been in touch with her doctor who was waiting to give Chrissie a sedative. This had little immediate effect, and Chrissie sat with Ann and Joe in their sitting-room, drinking cup after cup of tea and praying. Donny phoned the police, who were now at the club, to find out what was happening.

Ten years later, Chrissie recalled for me what happened next as if only a few hours had elapsed.

'Pat went out of the room to put the kettle on again. We'd drunk gallons of tea by then. The next thing I knew was Pat and Donny were standing in the doorway. Pat said to him: "I think you'd better tell your Mummy now."

'I looked up at Donny. Donny said to me: "I'm sorry Mummy. Your prayers are just a waste of time. Freddie is dead."'

Considering the interval between Freddie's death and my talking to her, Chrissie Mills was amazingly clear about the times of events. Others who were there that night were far less precise. Indeed, as we will see in Chapter 12, it is impossible to lay down a definite timetable for what had happened at the club and in Goslett Yard from the time Mills drove up and parked until Chrissie saw those bloodstains on her white suit jacket.

At the inquest, the statements made by the head-waiter, the doorman and the joint proprietor make interesting, if confusing, reading. For long periods it is impossible to establish exactly what Mills was doing or where he was. Why did it take so long for anyone to realize that he had collapsed? Why did two employees, both of whom had shaken him, fail to see the extensive bloodstains but notice that there was froth about his lips? Photographs taken after his death show the bloodstains . . . the body doesn't bleed *after* death, so the blood should have been evident earlier on to anyone coming close to him. Two employees shook Mills as he slumped in the back of the car; both went back to the club and told the joint proprietor that they'd been unable to wake him. Why did Andy Ho, a long-time friend of Mills, wait so long before sending for an ambulance? Did he want to get Chrissie's permission before taking action? Why did he not go out himself to try and wake his friend?

The coroner's verdict was that Freddie Mills had taken his own life, but those who knew him well have never accepted this verdict. As young Susan Mills told her mother: 'Whatever the situation facing Daddy may have been, I'll never believe it. He loved us far too much. We knew him. The police and all those other people didn't.'

# 2

To reach an informed opinion as to whether Freddie Mills committed suicide or was murdered, it is necessary to consider not only the published facts – the circumstances of his death as issued by the police – but also the social atmosphere and ambiance of the years during which the famous fighter fought, survived, and finally became a show-business character, if never a star.

The late '50s and the '60s were the days of gang warfare. The Kray twins ruled north of the Thames whilst the Richardson brothers were kings on the south bank. Corruption flourished even among the highest-ranking police officers, especially at the Yard. A large proportion of those responsible for enforcing the law received regular back-handers from the very villains they were meant to be apprehending and putting away.

Afternoon drinking-clubs, usually sited in the basements of dingy side-streets, were mushrooming. Night-spots were raking in the gold, even if the hostesses were losing out on their after-work takings to the keen amateurs who were now in competition with them. Musicals filled the West End theatres. Pop-singers became famous overnight and reverted to being nonentities almost as speedily. Even City men were abandoning staid pin-stripes for more exotic patterns and colours. Teenagers thought themselves free of former restraints even while they loitered on the street corners in gangs trying to conceal their individual inadequacies. Youth did rebel, but with flowers, whilst the Beatles composed their anthems. The '60s were swinging and unrepressed, the Pill had launched the Permissive Society. Whereas sex had been a topic outlawed at middle-class dinner-tables, conversations were now almost totally uninhibited. Girls who in previous decades would have been struggling to preserve their virginities now felt guilty and out of the swim if they hadn't lost them by fifteen.

The boxing industry also deteriorated . . . if that were possible. Boxing has always been a magnet for the shadier sections of the community, but the exploitation of fighters now became subtler than before. Fights were seldom fixed, but the combatants were manipulated so that the results suited the pockets of the promoters and big-time gamblers. Jovial Jack Solomons, the former fishmonger from the East End who'd been borne to power on the broad shoulders of Boy Boon, the lightweight from Chatteris, bestrode the boxing world, only occasionally challenged by hawk-nosed Harry-the-Horse Levene; a character who might have stepped straight out of a Damon Runyon story.

From the Bayswater Road, along Park Lane, via Shepherds' Market up to the 'Dilly, the Messina Brothers wove their grotty but profitable web of vice. West End pimps had to chip in or risk being slashed.

There was already a strong Chinese presence in the Gerrard Street area of the West End, but then, as now, the Chinese community there was largely concerned with restaurants and retail food shops: the Triads were not known at that time. However, in dockland the traditional Eastern vices of gambling and dope flourished: two of the most successful illicit Chinese clubs were not two hundred yards from the Aldgate Pump. Intellectual white food-connoisseurs made a conversational topic of their regular visits to the Old Friends in East India Dock Road. This was the real London China Town, an area that white gangsters left well alone. The Chinese Godfathers looked to wider horizons and were beginning to be dissatisfied with preying on their own people; smoky gambling clubs were gradually spreading Westward.

We are all products of our genes, environments and cultural ambiances. Freddie Mills had been uprooted from the refined, if geriatric, air of Bournemouth, his home town, and tossed into the rough world of the boxing-booths. He fought all comers in fairgrounds, drill-halls, town halls and skating-rinks. His pounding fists and apparent imperviousness to punishment carried him from four- and six-rounders until he was topping bills all over the country. Eventually he reached the apex of his profession when he defeated Gus Lesnevich for the championship of the world.

Mills was a colourful, exciting fighter. He had little of Len Harvey's skill, but what he lacked in art and craft he more than made up for with aggression. Jack Solomons, as shrewd as a weasel, exploited this talent, not hesitating to toss him into the ring against world-class fighters who were stones heavier than himself. With Freddie Mills topping the bill, the promoter was guaranteed success, and no promoter will argue against profits, even at the expense of a boxer's health.

We have to ask whether all those blows to the head suffered in these over-weight matches might have damaged Mills's brain. Certainly he showed no overt symptoms of punch-drunkenness when, after retirement, he strutted on to the stage or appeared on TV as a feed for comics.

Freddie Mills had a great lust for life. He relished good company, and would even put up with dull people so long as they cheered him. He had been hero-worshipped since his late teens. Every time he visited the Windmill Street gymnasium from which Solomons ran his tournaments, it would be like the arrival of the Pied Piper, and he would have to brush off a retinue of teenage fans before he could talk business with the promoter. Even the men queuing across the street for front seats at the 'never-closing' Windmill Theatre would stop drooling for a few seconds to wish him luck. When Freddie hung up his gloves, it was only natural he should turn to show-business. No London boxing tournament was complete unless Freddie was introduced from the ring before the main contest.

On his wave of popularity, he bought a Chinese restaurant, and when it began to lose money he converted it into a night-club. There, every evening, he would chat with the members, who usually insisted on having their photographs taken with their arms around the ex-champion's neck.

Few of those who clamoured round Freddie Mills realized he suffered from dizzy spells and fits of depression. Outwardly, he appeared the stereotype of the successful extrovert.

Physically, from early youth Freddie Mills had had everything in his favour. He was strong, fit and without a superfluous pound on his body. His face was rugged and cheerful, with alert eyes which met any questioning gaze unflinchingly. On my first meeting with him, what most struck me were his craggy eyebrows which jutted from his forehead like the furze of a cliff-top concealing the entrance to a cave. They might have been designed by nature as a natural protection from punches for his eyeballs.

For professional boxers to retain their looks after a dozen or so contests is rare indeed. Few fighters resemble the traditional Roman gladiator, eagle-eyed and aquiline-nosed. Freddie Mills's nose certainly wasn't straight, for by the time he was out of his teens it had been broken several times. How could it have been otherwise? The most skilful boxer – and not even Freddie with his unbounded confidence in himself claimed to be a boxing artist – cannot prevent every punch getting through his defence, and Freddie, in his days at the boxing-booth, often had to face six or seven challengers in the space of an afternoon. But though crooked his nose wasn't spread all over his face as is frequently the case with boxers of his style.

His other outstanding features were the two deeply etched furrows which ran down his cheeks on either side of his nose. These ruts divided his face into two separate planes, which, with his prominent chin, suggested that the whole central section had been added by nature as an afterthought.

Because he was so solidly built, Freddie never gave the impression of being tall even though he was almost six foot. His twelve stone six pounds – his natural fighting weight – were well distributed on his strong frame, and although he had a puncher's powerful shoulders he didn't give the appearance of being muscle-bound.

Although Freddie had been a boxer since his early teens and must have seen many examples of the deviousness of managers and promoters, he still retained a rather touching belief in man's innate honesty. He wanted to believe the best of everyone. Yet that isn't to suggest he was naive: it was just an example of the triumph of hope over experience.

After Mills's death, I asked Jack Solomons how Freddie could have left such a meagre sum – less than £400 – when his fists had earned him hundreds of thousands. Solomons, like all good managers, could bear boxers' misfortunes with stoicism. He shrugged off any responsibility. 'Tony, if Freddie was short of cash he knew he could always come to me. I'd always have put my hand into my pocket for him. If his club was crashing I'd have staked him to start again without question.'

(Such words are usually cheap. Boy Boon had lifted Jack Solomons from being a small-time promoter at the Devonshire Club to being the king of British boxing. Once he was no longer a drawing-card for Solomons, Boon was finally reduced to fighting six-rounders for small purses in Australia. His punch had gone and he was being routinely outpointed. I once told Jack Solomons that I thought this was a tragic end for a great fighter. Solomons lit a new Havana cigar before answering. 'Boon was an idiot. I did everything for him. When he went broke I even gave him £500 out of my own pocket.' At the time Solomons was already a multi-millionaire.)

In the immediate post-war years, I became an inspector of the British Boxing Board of Control. I was brought into this industry by my closest friend, James Dilwyn James, who at the time was the official doctor as well as being a steward of the controlling body. Jimmy was a tremendous amateur middleweight who could have made a fortune had he turned to the professional ranks. However he preferred the flesh-pots to training.

Besides, he was working full-time in the pathology department of University College Hospital before becoming head of the blood transfusion service for North London, from Edgware Hospital. Jimmy loved boxing, and respected boxers as much as I did. He also hated the way boxers were exploited and treated as mere commodities by the parasites of the business, and he suggested I should join him in an attempt to keep the sport as clean as possible. Today I believe this to be impossible: the scales are weighted against the reformer, and I think boxing should be banned.

When a world-championship contest was promoted, two inspectors were allocated to ensure that neither fighter was 'nobbled'. I found myself as Mills's inspector for both of his contests against Gus Lesnevich. Freddie lost the first, his non-stop aggression unable to put the American off his stride. The return was totally different. Freddie had clearly learned from his mistakes, and instead of crowding forward with no thought to defence, he stood upright and used a classic left lead. After the final bell, he was carried round the ring by his excited supporters. Certainly this was his greatest hour. I was borne back with him by the crush to his dressing-room. Every time we met after that he'd refer to that evening. He relived it again and again.

Freddie and I enjoyed each other's company. We shared a relish for life. But although we laughed a lot together, I wasn't blind to his main weakness: he took almost a childish pleasure in popularity. Today, I regret I never took the trouble to delve beneath his hail-fellow-well-met exterior to see if, perhaps, there wasn't another Mills, a more remote and more interesting person who hid his feelings from the world. Mills was the champion of the world; he was a showbiz personality; he was a man who expanded under applause; he was also intensely selfish and clearly wasn't really interested in his fellow man's troubles or emotions – that was my judgement.

After his death I was amazed to learn he had been a Samaritan. In his role of counsellor, I learned, he was sometimes concerned with talking would-be suicides out of taking their own lives. Apparently he gave up being a Samaritan after the death of his dear friend, ballad-singer Michael Holliday. When Holliday killed himself, Freddie didn't try to conceal his tears from the club members. Shortly afterwards, as I learned from his family, he suffered from a severe depression. I had never suspected that this gregarious, outgoing man had suffered from black devils on his shoulder.

After he'd hung up his gloves, Freddie was for a time quite successful in the entertainment world. He was a 'safe' guest, nothing if not predictable, always with a ready smile and an ideal 'feed'. Nevertheless, he found making a living from the boards difficult. Fortunately, he didn't have to depend on his show-business fees. Advised by his friend Bill Bavin, he'd invested in property, and owned several houses and flats in Greenwich. He'd also gone into the restaurant trade with Andy Ho, a friend who'd assured him he knew everything about catering. But although all the arguments for going into the entertainment world were strong, he was a child stepping out into a jungle.

For many years the West End of London had been accepted as an area of some refinement; a place of fashion, tailoring, restaurants and luxury hotels. Stores with household names and holding the royal charter competed for the best sites in the world; the famous thoroughfares of Regent Street, Bond Street, Park Lane and Oxford Street. Yet by the '50s one square mile of the West End had become the centre of London's organized vice: in the streets round Soho Square strip-joints, sex shops, illicit gambling clubs and clandestine brothels proliferated. Most of these Soho clubs were seedy, dank and dark – indeed, their sordidness was part of their perverse attraction. In these dimly lit basements, visitors from overseas and businessmen from the North jostled to be fleeced; they were almost like sacrifices climbing upon the altar to be killed. They shelled out wads of notes to indulge their fantasies without danger of being identified.

These clubs drew to the square bounded by Oxford Street, Shaftesbury Avenue, Regent Street and Charing Cross Road not only those bent on a night out, but also tourists, sightseers and voyeurs who came not to take part but to ogle, gloat, fantasize and disapprove. Many entrepreneurs planning to open new clubs in this golden mile couldn't find suitable premises because the competition was so hot. They had to accept second best and rent rooms in neighbouring streets and alleys. These ventures were seldom successful: they would enjoy a brief spell of popularity as the debs and Johnnies eagerly tried any new joint. Then they would fade and close.

Goslett Yard is only a few yards outside the main Soho complex, but even those few yards meant that a club sited there failed to be seen by the rubbernecks. The main entrance to Mills's restaurant and later night spot was just out of the limelight. Charing Cross Road is a bastard road, without the panache of Regent Street or Bond Street, or the attractive seediness of Greek Street or Dean Street. There are no smart men's clothing shops, no fashion houses, no sex shops or peepshows. Instead there are second-hand clothing shops, bookshops and shabby offices from which employment agents tout for waiters and kitchen-hands. No wonder Freddie Mills's catering ventures weren't successful.

Freddie had the popularity and the ability to make club members welcome . . . but his presence alone wasn't enough to fill the tables.

# 3

Although this was an age of violence and corruption, it was also a time of important social advance. The Second World War had dented, if not destroyed, the age-old class divisions. Beveridge had erected a signpost pointing to a brave new world, and the NHS was the flagship of the post-war generation.

But whilst it is necessary to understand the social environment so as to see the backcloth to the Mills tragedy, it is also vital to appreciate how his profession – boxing – was run. It is also, of course, necessary to know about Mills's upbringing and family background – indeed all the factors which moulded his character – if one is to be able to think oneself into Mills's mind. Without this preparation, how can one imagine how Mills would have reacted to all the sensational rumours which were circulating in the months before his death?

For instance, how would he have answered to any suggestion that he was about to be accused of homosexual practices? If his club were going out of business and he were facing bankruptcy, would he have been likely to give up or would he have shrugged those hefty shoulders and gone to work as a navvy until he had amassed enough capital to start again? There is little doubt that if his debts had been weighing on his mind, he could have borrowed from within the boxing and theatre fraternities to tide him over the stormy days. One must also ask oneself what his reaction would have been to racketeers' threats? Would he have caved in, or shown that courage he'd always displayed when facing a Goliath in the ring?

And what of the supporting players in the drama of Mills's death? Their descriptions of what happened must also be judged in the context of their times and their characters. Would the club staff have been terrified and handed in their notices if they had been told that gangsters were threatening Mills and his family? Would fear have caused them to jettison their loyalty to their employer and cover up for murder? If the club had closed, they would have been out of work – but at the time there were plenty of jobs for doormen and bouncers in Soho clubs.

The whole of Freddie Mills's life had been lived within the grubby world of crime. How could it have been otherwise when boxing has always reeked of corruption?

Boxing is a sport – or perhaps 'industry' would be the more appropriate world – with its own jargon and clichés. These are often contradictory; frequently ill-founded. 'The bigger they are the harder they fall,' is the inevitable rejoinder to 'A good big 'un will always beat a good little 'un.' Probably the most ironic and cynical of all such clichés is 'the noble art of self-defence'. Boxing is seldom noble, and if boxers concentrated on self-defence the halls would be empty.

The boxing supporter is probably the only sports follower who has never participated in any way in his chosen sport – ninety-nine per cent of those who throng the ring-side, howling abuse, have never pulled on a pair of boxing-gloves, and nothing on earth would persuade them to climb through the ropes.

The sixty-five-year-old ring-sider with tortoise-wrinkled neck and chewed cigar-butt dangling from loose lips will yell 'Charlie!' or 'Yellow bastard!' in contempt for a sixteen-year-old youth trembling with fright as he is stretched upon the canvas. The dinner-jacketed businessman sipping his brandy at the ringside of the sporting club after a good dinner will shout to the boxer whom he's backed: 'Be first!' He won't know enough about his 'boy' to realize that he is a counter-puncher and must wait for the opponent to lead if he's to score.

Many of the boxing clichés have their origins in the prize ring. 'Toeing the line' is a relic of the bare-knuckle fights when men fought until one of them was carried bloody and unconscious back to the corner. If he failed to recover enough to 'toe the line' or 'come up to scratch' he was declared the loser. The aristocracy and gentry were always more than ready to wager vast sums that their men could successfully face any challenge. Whether the proposed match was fair or whether the odds were that their man would end close to death, never troubled their minds. It wasn't a pretty scene, but in some ways it was better than what was to follow – at least the Corinthians were interested in the reputations of their boxers, if not their health. The ex-champion was a respected character and was often financed by his patron so he could open an inn on retirement. After boxing became an industry, ex-champions were thrown on the scrap-heap as worthless commodities.

Like any other industry, boxing today has its various levels of management. At the top are the promoters and entrepreneurs. Middle-management consists of the officials of the British Boxing Board of Control, the managers, trainers and matchmakers. (It has to be faced that the Board only exists by kind permission of the top men who put up the money.) The factory-floor level is the area occupied by the boxers, whips and minor officials.

In the days of bare-knuckle fighting, the ring was usually pitched in an open field deep in the countryside and remote from police interference. The venue was kept secret until the day of the contest. When the Benicia Boy, John Carmel Heenan, challenged Englishman Tom Sayers on 17 April 1860, three trains left London for unknown destinations. En route, the police lined platforms of stations with their sabres drawn ready to prevent passengers alighting at their town if that should be the destination. (In view of boxing's shady reputation, it is amusing to note that the Benicia Boy's direct descendant, also John Carmel Heenan, became a cardinal and head of the Catholic Church in the United Kingdom.)

Tournaments today are far from secret: they are widely advertised. The promoters daily give out to the press highly coloured tales emphasizing the hatred existing between the two boxers and the certainty that one or the other will suffer grave damage. Instead of rings being pitched in fields or behind coaching inns, fights are staged in town halls, swimming baths and concert halls. For decades the Royal Albert Hall has been a favourite boxing venue, maybe because its giant organ can drown the jeers of the disappointed fight-fans.

Between the wars in the United States, gangsters openly boasted of 'owning a boy' or 'part of a boy'. The part mentioned was invariably the part which fought and earned money, not the part which ate and cost money to keep. Champion boxers earned peanuts compared with the vast purses of today. Only the promoters and their backers made big money. If a boxer publicly complained of unfair treatment, the odds were that his already scarred face would suffer further damage. The gangsters decided who should fight whom, where they should fight, and, in many cases, who would win. Boxers 'dived' to order. It was safer to obey instructions.

Here we also had our gangsters though they never operated on anything like the scale of the States. Spivs and racing racketeers managed to hold licences as promoters and managers, but 'fixed fights' were still rare. It was far easier to manipulate the odds by over-matching a boy early in his career or accepting a substitute contest when the manager knew his boy couldn't be fit in time. A boxer could be matched at a weight below his best and so have to lose pounds at the last moment. This would weaken him, so again the odds would be manipulated. The much rumoured 'dives' were more fiction than fact, for boxers aren't good actors and the more knowledgeable fight-fans are quick to detect a fix.

The British Boxing Board of Control is a self-elected, self-perpetuating organization. In the past, promoters, managers, boxers and trainers decided which of their fellows should be allowed licences. There were disadvantages to this democratic system: most of the Board members owed their livings to promoters and so tended to follow where those with the money pointed. Later, because of this, the non-financially-interested were invited to join the Board, but this has resulted in rule by the ignorant. The stewards of the Board are without doubt honourable men, but, with a couple of exceptions, they are mere babes when it comes to the inner workings of the sport. Onslow Fane, a former chairman of the Board and Old Etonian, was often compared to the pianist in the brothel who never knew what was going on upstairs, and today the general position is much the same. Those who pay the piper – the promoters – are the real tsars. They may fight amongst themselves; but without them there would be no boxing.

The villains who infested the industry between the wars didn't have to comb the highways and byways to find victims. There has always been a pool of starry-eyed youngsters queuing up to be martyred. Psychologists suggest it is not that beggars batten on the wealthy, it is generous donors who actually seek out beggars, needing people to be dependent on them. This is very true of boxers and would-be boxers. The lad on the threshold of a boxing career is subconsciously searching for someone he can trust who will take all the mental worries off his shoulders. He is actually anxious to believe any manager who talks in hundreds of thousands and who promises to look after the boy as 'I'd look after my own son'. It is usually a waste of time for the more honest manager to try and warn the youngster of the pitfalls and physical and mental dangers unavoidable in the ring. Outside the dealing rooms of the City, there are today only four main ways that a lad in his late teens or early twenties can become a millionaire: singing, football, snooker, or boxing. No wonder kids of strong physiques and self-assurance have stars in their eyes as they contemplate wealthy futures. No wonder they are deaf to warnings!

Nevertheless, despite the rackets and the exploitation, a small number of boxers manage to keep their reputations untainted, their brains unscrambled and their pockets unpicked. They are few. Usually they have to be men of outstanding courage, physique and, sadly, of limited intelligence. Mickey Duff, an ex-top-class boxer and the most powerful figure in British boxing since the demise of Jack Solomons, stated on tape in my programme, *The Purse*: 'After all, they were never going to be brain surgeons, were they?'

To be a champion boxer, a man has to have intense pride in himself and be a man who would prefer to go down to bloody defeat rather than be accused of 'swallowing it', a boxing term for staying down for the full count when you could have got up.

Freddie Mills was such a man. He always said, 'I'll fight till I drop.' And so he did. Every person who bought a ticket for a Mills contest knew he would get his money's worth.

When Jack Solomons promoted the Freddie Mills v. Joey Maxim contest for the world crown, he sent Ted Broadribb, Mills's manager, to the United States to negotiate terms with Maxim's mentor, Jack Curwin. Broadribb came home delighted with himself for making what he believed to be a good deal. However, going through the small print Solomons concluded that Broadribb had been diddled and had promised Maxim too large a percentage. Broadribb and Solomons had previously talked about Mills's cut but had agreed nothing finally. Because of the deal Broadribb had made in the States, Solomons now proposed that Mills should receive a smaller percentage of the purse than his challenger; twenty-five per cent of the gate and ancillary rights. Broadribb demanded thirty per cent. Boxing negotiations are similar to those conducted between employers and trade-union representatives. The leader of the employers offers ten pounds less than he is really prepared to pay; the union spokesman demands ten pounds more than he is prepared to accept. Then after long, windy discussions, they gradually draw closer together until they reach agreement. Sir Peter Parker, former king of British Rail, has described management/union negotiations as a 'rehearsed dance'.

Both Ted Broadribb and Jack Solomons were experienced negotiators. Eventually, after fierce arguments and many threats that the fight would have to be abandoned, they shook hands on a deal. Mills would receive twenty-seven and a half per cent. Solomons, of course, emphasized: 'It's two and a half per cent more than I can afford to pay . . . I shall lose on the show, I'm only going on with it to keep faith with the public. Jack Solomons is a man of his word . . . and I've promised this fight to the fight-fans. But I shall lose money.' Promoters can bring tears to all but the most cynical eyes when talking about losing money.

The following day the world champion strode into Jack Solomons' office in Windmill Street.

'I understand, Jack, that you had an argument with the Old Man yesterday.'

Solomons spread his hands expressively as if to say, 'It wasn't my doing.'

Mills threw the signed contract on to the desk. 'Well, I'm not having it. Make out a fresh contract for twenty-five per cent. That's what I'd have taken . . . and let's not have any more argy-bargy about it!'

Generously, Solomons gave way. The promoter could always find good reasons for making money.

It was a typical reaction on the part of Freddie Mills. This was no isolated example; no sudden attack of altruism. Mills was no fool. He knew that despite all Solomons' talk of losing money, the promoter was on to a 'good thing'. The fight had caught the imagination of the public and every seat would be sold. Solomons would still be able to afford his Corona-size Havana cigars. But as far as Mills was concerned Ted Broadribb was his – Mills's – manager and as such had agreed to paying Maxim too much, so Mills felt responsible, and he didn't want to be in debt to any man.

Mills was essentially uncomplicated. He wanted to feel needed, to be respected and to be liked . . . He worried continually about what people might think of him. In the ring he had self-confidence verging on the arrogant, but outside it he had more than a trace of humility.

Boxing is the only sport in which the sole aim of the sportsman is to render his fellow unconscious. In wrestling, accidents can happen and bones may be broken, but inflicting physical harm on your opponent isn't the prime objective. The intent is to pin him to the canvas by superior skill or strength. Professional wrestlers cannot afford to put each other out of work. There are no such restrictions for boxers.

Boxing supporters seldom tire of proclaiming how they enjoy watching contests between skilled men. They lie. Every promoter knows only too well – usually from painful financial experience – that if he features only skilled boxers, as opposed to blood-and-thunder thumpers, the halls will be empty. The contest between boxer and puncher attracts because there is the excitement of hoping that the puncher will get through the skilled boxer's defence and floor him. Every supporter knows that however far ahead on points one fighter may be, a single punch can still end the contest. But the real crowd-puller is two Goliaths taking great swipes at each other. The knowledge that any punch, however wild, may cause immediate unconsciousness, is the magnet. Many of the most famous fights have been between flyweights . . . but it is the giants which, in showbiz parlance, 'put bums on seats'. Boxing fans want to see blood or knock-outs: it's as simple as that.

Freddie Mills wasn't an artist of the ring; not what is known as a 'Fancy Dan'. He was a slugger; a non-stop fighter whose appearance on a bill foreordained drama. He scorned the subtle manoeuvre; the sidestep and the combination punch were niceties for which he had little patience. Mills lived for the moment. His chin sunk deep between his shoulders – often his sole tactic for self-protection – he would plod inexorably forward, punching, swinging, hacking and chopping until he either KO'd his opponent or forced the referee to stop the contest. When he won the lightheavyweight championship of the world from American Gus Lesnevich, who only two years earlier had knocked him out four seconds from the end of the contest, the crowd was astounded when Mills elected to box rather than fight. For the first time they saw Mills use a classic straight left, block and ride punches. Indeed, he used a straight left in very much the same way as Lesnevich had used it to beat him at their first encounter. No one, till then, had realized or even suspected that Mills could box. By instinct he had always been a fighter.

But clever boxing could never have won Freddie Mills the popularity he so much enjoyed. It was his recklessness and readiness to accept punches so he could get within distance to drive his own blows home, that endeared him to the fans. The spectator could identify himself personally with the beetle-browed swashbuckler. In that private dream which most of us use to offset our grey lives, we could imagine we were Mills. We could be in the ring throwing punches, scorning risks and taunting our opponents. The clown traditionally yearns to play Hamlet: for the average fighting-fan, Freddie was the hero. He broke every rule of classic boxing . . . and still won.

'The only good fighter is a hungry one' is another boxing cliché. Usually it is true. A man must be ruthless to become a champion. He mustn't hesitate when he sees his opponent is staggering but must throw everything into the blow that will end the contest. When he notices the thin line of blood below his opponent's eye, he mustn't pay heed to any finer feelings but direct his hardest punches to the wounded area. Such ruthlessness is often sharpened by deprivation.

The man with a gentler, more privileged background, who as a teenager has always eaten well, may have reflexes as quick as the poverty-reared fighter. He may well be more intelligent and quicker-witted. But inevitably the moment comes when he is unable to avoid a heavy punch. Suddenly he finds himself on the canvas. Through clouds of near unconsciousness, he'll become aware of those leering, jeering faces pressing forward for a closer view, of the roar for blood . . . his blood – the roar of the Roman crowd giving the thumbs down for a stricken gladiator. At this moment he may well ask himself: 'Why should I drag myself to my feet? What for? To give excitement to these swine?'

But the man who in childhood has had to go without food and has had to fight every day to survive will look up from the canvas with real hatred. Afterwards in the dressing-room, he may laugh and console his recent opponent, but during those seconds of humiliation, his whole concentration will be geared towards revenge.

Most great champions have been hungry fighters. This is the reason that for stretches of twenty years or so at a time a particular ethnic group has seemed to rule the boxing world. At the turn of this century the most successful boxers were of Irish origin. They came from the slums of Dublin and the hovels of Cork and Donegal, leaving grimy back streets where there was no work to go out into the world, angry and resentful. Their fists were their only weapons against grinding poverty. Such a man was James J. Braddock, the Cinderella Man, who went straight from the dole queue to defeat the glamorous Max Baer for the world's heavyweight championship. The Irish emigrated in their thousands and wherever they settled boxing flourished. Though Liverpool and Glasgow became famous boxing nurseries, the boxers there weren't English and Scots . . . they were nearly all of Irish ancestry.

In London of pre-war years, the hungry fighters were from the alleyways and dank yards of the East End. Most of them were Jewish, and almost every one of them was living in what today we would describe as 'conditions below subsistence level'. The most famous of them were world champions, Ted Kid Lewis and Yiddle Kid Berg. There were many others who might equally justifiably have worn world crowns had they been in the right place at the right time: Al Phillips, the Aldgate Tiger, Harry Mason, Dave Finn, Harry Mizler, Harry Lazer and durable Alby Hollister who almost destroyed the blossoming career of Randy Turpin, a boxer who was to take his own life.

Kid Lewis never wore shoes until he was ten years old. He seldom had enough to eat. In the ring his body looked as if he were a famine victim, his ribs standing out like xylophone keys. His face was so pallid that he looked as if he were suffering from pernicious anaemia. But however fragile he might appear from the ringside, he would drive relentlessly forward. He was tough and ruthless, motivated by real hatred for anyone who stood between him and winning. As a boy he had led the Jewish lads through a daily gauntlet of punches and kicks from the Goy children who had been raised to be anti-Semitic by their 'Christian' parents. Having fought from an early age with fists, teeth and feet, he had little fear for a gloved opponent. He once told me: 'Tony, I'm an amiable guy, but when I'm in the ring I really hate!'

A decade later, Wales became the nursery of British boxing. Miners are tough, proud people. When they struck against inhuman conditions and meagre pay in the early years of the century, the pit owners brought in blacklegs whilst the police beat up those on the picket lines. The middle-class public misunderstood – or didn't care to find out – the reasons for the rebellion of the pitmen; strange-speaking, scarred men. The Welsh valleys fostered exactly the right conditions to produce boxers: poverty and hatred. Wee Jimmy Wilde, the Ghost with a Hammer in his Hands, ruled the flyweight division in the first quarter of the century even though he was a full stone below the eight-stone limit. Wilde's worst defeat was against an American stones heavier than himself who came into the ring pounds over the scheduled weight. Wilde fought only because the Prince of Wales requested him to do so. Wilde suffered the blows, not his royal patron.

The classic Welsh boxer was represented by 'Peerless' Jim Driscoll who was also lionized by royalty, though they did nothing to help him after he hung up his gloves. Driscoll died from the effects of starving himself to make the weight. And there were many others: Tom Thomas, Gypsy Daniels, Fred Dyer – the Singing Boxer – and, more recently, Tonypandy Tommy Farr. Jack Petersen, a lion-hearted lightheavy-weight, could have been world champion if he'd stuck to his own weight, but, sadly, greedy management threw him in with men far too heavy. Petersen eventually became President of the British Boxing Board of Control.

Wherever there is dire poverty, there are fighting men. This is as true today as it ever was. Over many years black Americans, descendants of African slaves, have provided the majority of world champions. The first world heavyweight champion was Jack Johnson, who, when he fought for the championship, was played into the ring with 'All Niggers Look Alike to Me'. The fight-fans were infuriated when Johnson struck back by openly boasting of his affairs with white women. Perhaps the most respected of heavyweight champions was the Sepia Slayer, Joe Louis. Louis, a great sportsman, was to be grossly exploited so that he was not only robbed of almost every dollar his fists had earned, but ended his days in a mental home, having been confined to an invalid chair for more than ten years.

There has been a host of fine black fighters: Jersey Joe Walcott, Sugar Ray Robinson, Ike Williams, Henry 'Buzz' Armstrong, Sugar Ray Leonard, Marvellous Marvin Hagler, Joe Frazier, George Foreman and, of course, 'the Greatest' – Cassius Clay, later Muhammad Ali. Yet even the Greatest was a victim of his sport. Within ten years of hanging up his gloves, he had become a shambling, shuffling, inarticulate wreck.

In the days when he could still string words together, Ali told Alan Hubbard of the *Observer*:

The masses of people, black and white, are poor in America. That's why they root for me and make me their favourite. They don't have nothin'. The things I say and the things I do . . . they love me for it. I'm their warrior who stands up for them and bucks the system.

You hear them at fights: 'Ali, Ali, Ali . . . Kick their asses.' They all want to see me come back and kick the shit out of whoever I'm fighting.

Until quite recent years there was still a colour-bar in British boxing. Black Manuel Abrew from Leith was described on fight bills as The Unofficial Scottish Heavyweight Champion . . . even though he'd beaten the white Scottish champion. On his first visit to London to fight at the York Hall, Bethnal Green, he remembered hearing howls from the gallery of 'Kill the black bastard!' Late in his life he told me: 'I kept looking round the hall for this black bastard. At first I didn't realize it was me. When I did I was terrified. I'd never met such hatred in Scotland.' His widow, Clementine, saw Manuel lose the sight of one eye and his brother become totally blind through boxing. She says today: 'There's no excuse for civilized man to try and injure his fellow. Boxing is a brutal sport and should be banned.'

Many of the American black fighters came from the cotton fields of the South or the back alleys of the industrial cities. Many also learned their boxing in penitentiaries, where the sport was looked on as a safety valve. Today the street gangs in the USA are the nurseries in which the fight managers find their boys. Gus D'Amato knew he'd struck gold when he found the barrel-necked Mike Tyson, and as long as D'Amato lived Tyson, despite a wild nature, was undefeatable.

Freddie Mills was the exception to the rule in that he didn't have a background of poverty nor come from a deprived area. He didn't have to fight in back alleys for survival. He didn't know what it was like to go without food or to do without shoes. On the contrary, he was born and brought up in the outskirts of Bournemouth, that almost too-respectable south-coast seaside resort where retired colonels, former presidents of the Women's Institute and elderly vicars are more common than muggers, gangsters and hoodlums.

This is not to suggest that the Mills family was well-to-do or middle class. It wasn't. But they certainly weren't poverty-stricken. Freddie's father was a rag-and-bone merchant, and though he wasn't wealthy his family wanted for nothing. Freddie was always well fed and neatly dressed. His home was comfy, his childhood secure. He was surrounded by love and affection.

Mills certainly had no reason to rail against the Fates; no reason to hate the world or his fellow man. He had none of the bitterness and hatred which often motivates fighters, yet he was so successful in his chosen profession that he became the first Briton to win the world's lightheavyweight crown. (Boxing historians will undoubtedly recall that Ruby Bob Fitzsimmons, a Cornishman, had held that title fifty years earlier. However, Fitzsimmons left these shores when he was only two years old and learned all his fighting in Australia.)

As a teenager, Mills was always day-dreaming of fame and fortune. An ardent cinema fan, he realized from quite a young age that he could never become another Laurence Olivier or Cary Grant but that, if luck smiled on him, he might make his name in the ring. Unlike many fighters, he never had to face parental disapproval when he told them he had decided to become a professional boxer. Indeed his father and his brothers encouraged him and were among his most ardent followers.

Yet the brutality of the prize-ring was alien to his character. He told George Whiting of the *Evening Standard* when he was a champion:

Deep down I have to fight myself before I can fight anyone else. It's been that way since I started in the booths right up to the time I fought Gus Lesnevich for the championship. I don't like hurting people and I like people hurting me even less. I'm dead scared when I see the other bloke sitting in his corner waiting to get up and clout me . . .

Was this frightened, self-conscious man the real Freddie Mills? In this interview was Mills trying to show what a modest man he was to curry sympathy, or was he lifting the mask most us wear to hide our personal doubts? Mills's passion for being liked and applauded stemmed from his self-doubts, if that statement to George Whiting is to be believed. The extrovert is often an innately shy person who has had to fight to overcome anxiety. Freddie Mills was extremely likeable; he would do anything for anybody . . . so long as he was allowed to hog the limelight. Few knew that he suffered from severe bouts of depression.

# 4

PSYCHOLOGISTS claim that traumas inflicted on us in our mothers' wombs affect our characters and personalities. Indeed, some believe that under hypnosis people can remember a time as much as three weeks before their birth. Certainly our relationships with our parents and those about us in our early years mould our adulthoods. The infant is father to the man.

We cannot know today whether Mrs Mills suffered any major shock whilst carrying her second son, or what influences there were on the young Freddie Mills in childhood, but without doubt there were contradictions in his character.

Outside the ring, he was affable, easy-going and greeted everyone he met as a potential friend. At first meeting you wondered if his geniality was genuine, or whether he was two-faced. He wasn't. As he rose in the boxing ranks he would have realized that the very people who cheered him so enthusiastically and swore that they had laid their last five pounds on him to win had, in all likelihood, wagered heavily on his opponent knocking him out. But if he felt contempt for them, he never allowed it to show. He wanted to think the best of everyone.

Inside the roped square, however, Freddie Mills had the arrogance which is essential for a champion. When he sensed his opponent might be weakening, he'd attack with all the ferocity of a wild animal. He gave and asked no quarter. He was a born fighter.

Boxing is a savage occupation. A far higher percentage of professional boxers have had criminal backgrounds than those in any other trade or profession. This fact contrasts starkly with the conventional view of the pro-boxing lobby that boxing provides a safety valve for frustrated young men and so prevents many of them turning to crime.

An analysis of today's leading fighters shows that many boxers learned their trade while serving prison sentences, often for crimes of violence when running with youthful gangs of muggers. The independently minded Freddie Mills, too, fell foul of authority at an early age, but his offence couldn't have been less villainous. In his autobiography, *Twenty Years*, he describes how, when he was ten, he was arraigned before the juvenile bench for stealing a pair of rollerskates from an empty building. His father had to pay a £1 fine. That was his only brush with the law until after he had retired from the ring, when he was found guilty in the magistrates' court of serving drinks out of hours in his night-club. Again not a very heinous offence. It was more serious when later he and his partner Andy Ho were rumoured to be running a call-girl racket from their premises.

That first crime, stealing rollerskates, had a profound effect on his life, for, having paid the fine for his son, Mr Mills insisted Freddie should join the local youth club, hoping that would keep him out of any further trouble. The youth club had a boxing section, and from then on Freddie was the most regular of members. There he could try out the boxing moves he learned from his elder brother Charles when they sparred in the street.

There were four children in the family; three boys and a girl. Freddie was closest to his brother Charles, who was seven years the elder. When Mrs Mills bought Freddie two pairs of boxing gloves for his birthday, Charlie, already a moderately successful professional middleweight, took over teaching his younger brother the rudiments of their sport. Their ring was the pavement outside their house in Parkstone Road, Parkstone, a suburb of Bournemouth. Their ring light was the street lamp outside their front door.

At first, Charlie concentrated on footwork believing that a good stance is the foundation of boxing, whatever the subsequent style the boxer embraces. So Freddie was forbidden to throw any punches but had to shuffle backwards, forwards and sideways without losing his balance, following wherever Charles led.

Having learned to keep his feet well-spaced, he was next taught to hold his hands high so he could parry, feint and block blows without taking himself out of distance. Only when he was confident that Freddie had learned these lessons soundly did Charlie allow his young brother to unleash the punches he'd been longing to try out. Even then Freddie was frustrated, for instead of permitting him to thrash forward, punching with both hands, Charlie kept up a chant: 'Left . . . left . . . use your left. Straight . . . punch straight . . . left, use your left.'

Freddie didn't want to punch 'straight'. He wanted to tear in, swinging with both hands. But he was intelligent enough to realize that he needed to learn to box, even though he wanted to fight. Nineteen years later, when Freddie won the world championship, it was by using a classic straight left.

As they sparred in the open street, Charlie would try to be patient. But sometimes his younger brother's inability to hold his natural aggression in rein would irritate him and, believing that Freddie was intentionally forgetting everything he'd been told, he would administer a sharp rebuke with a left hook to the nose. But however hard the punch, Freddie would never take a step backward if he could help it.

From those very early days when Freddie was little more than a boy, Charlie realized his brother's potential. He knew that if Freddie were taught soundly and were fortunate enough to be steered by an intelligent manager who wouldn't sacrifice him for the quick buck, he could reach the very top of the boxing ladder. Freddie was brave and strong, with a vicious punch. Even more important, he was ambitious and determined. In boxing dedication is essential. Most champions have suffered defeat some time in their careers, and that first defeat may be the moment of truth from which some never recover. To survive, the would-be champion must put his disappointment firmly behind him and force himself not to lose confidence. Jack Dempsey, the Manassa Mauler, one of the greatest heavyweight champions of all time, was knocked out very early in his career. Far from deciding that he had no future in the ring, the ex-hobo fought even more viciously from then on, seeing every opponent as an enemy threatening his entire future.

Of course, sometimes defeat is inevitable, as when a youngster is overmatched against too heavy or too experienced an opponent. This is the moment when the good trainer takes over. Whilst the manager is probably saying, 'Bad luck, son', before heading to pick up the purse at the box office, the trainer must be there to offer support, reassurance and to reburnish his young charge's confidence. He must also help the defeated boxer analyse the mistakes he has made. If the boy doesn't understand why he lost, he'll repeat his errors and defeat will follow on defeat. The purses will get smaller and his name will drop to the bottom of the fight bills. No longer will he see his name on the left-hand side of the bill – where the promoter places the names of the boys he wants to win – but on the right-hand side. Without realizing it, the lad will soon become a 'ham-and-egger', a trial horse for the new up-and-coming fighters. He will talk of his future plans and how he is certain to become a champion without noticing the smirks behind the hands.

Mrs Mills was the only member of his family who was unenthusiastic about Freddie's progress in the ring; and her disapproval wasn't based on any sentimentality. She told Freddie unequivocally that she had enough to do running the house, keeping it clean and feeding them all, to have time to be their washerwoman. If they came home with bloodstained clothes or sweat-stained vests, they could do the washing themselves.

Mills was a better student of boxing than of classroom lessons. But a would-be professional fighter must eventually put theory into practice. Moves learned in training can be quickly forgotten under attack. When sparring, boxers can pause to discuss their latest exchange of blows. In a contest, one boxer may attack the other so relentlessly that the second fighter hasn't time to mount an attack on his own behalf. The counter-punch learned in training may well be 'left in the gymnasium'.

Mills was determined to have practical experience. Most weekday afternoons would find him hanging about outside the railings at the local school waiting for the senior boys to emerge. Ignoring how much bigger than him most of them were, he'd challenge any likely-looking youth to put on the gloves. At first, most of them would accept with amusement. After all, they were almost full-grown whilst he was only just into his teens. But few of them returned for a second helping. Freddie was incapable of understanding their reluctance. In similar circumstances he knew that he would be unable to sleep until he had avenged a defeat.

By the age of thirteen, Freddie Mills was totally obsessed with boxing. Whenever a boxing tournament was being staged at the Old Winter Garden in Bournemouth, he'd cycle into the town. He could seldom raise the price of a ticket, so would try to sneak in with the crowd. If detected and turned away, he'd go round to the back of the hall, climb over the iron banisters of the fire-escape and claw his way up on to the roof. There he would prise open the ventilating window and from this precarious eyrie would watch the fighters below.

Inevitably, one day the promoter spotted him. But instead of taking steps to keep the young lad out, he so admired the boy's enthusiasm and courage that he left him alone. However the police also realized what was going on and warned the promoter they would hold him responsible if the lad fell to his death. Instead of sending for Mills's father and asking him to keep his son under control, the promoter lay in wait for Freddie and caught him as he was descending.

'You enjoy risking your life, son?'

Freddie gazed down at the ground. 'I enjoy boxing.'

The promoter gave a half grin. 'You must do.' Then he put his hand under the boy's chin and raised his head until he could look directly into his eyes. 'Come down next week. We've a novice competition. The lads won't be much bigger than you and they'll only be a year or so older.'

The following week Mills took part in his first official contest. He won on a knock-out. The next week he boxed in the semi-finals, and again stopped his opponent. He won the final and was presented with a silver egg-cup by the local mayor.

The promoter was delighted with his protégé, but as a man who'd spent many years in boxing he knew the risks. The day after the final he sent Jack Turner, one of his boxing employees, to see Mills's father.

Turner advised Mr Mills: 'Your lad's a natural . . . a real natural. But boxing can be a bad game. Get him a job, and keep boxing as a hobby.' Mr Mills passed on the advice to his son, but the words were wasted. By then Freddie was determined that nothing would prevent his becoming a professional fighter.

When he was sixteen, his father sent him to work as a dairy-boy delivering pints of milk from a horse-drawn float. The milkman, who derived much pleasure from his boy's local boxing fame, sat on the float holding the reins while Freddie ran behind, breaking away every few seconds to dart up the path of a house to leave a bottle on the doormat. It was excellent roadwork. Gilbert Odd, one of the most knowledgeable of boxing writers, remembered Freddie Mills telling him that as he ran behind that float he'd escape into day-dreams and knock out Georges Carpentier, stop Battling Siki – giving the Senegalese fighter's tame leopard a clip for good luck – outpoint Gene Tunney and outpunch Jack Dempsey.

The promoter who had advised Freddie to treat boxing as a hobby saw that Freddie was determined to carry on fighting. So why shouldn't he benefit? After all, he had been the first to give the lad his chance in the ring. So once again Jack Turner was dispatched to talk to Mr Mills. Jack Turner was a big, red-faced man who had been a professional boxer and as a result had one glass eye, the unnatural glint in which was enough to inspire fear in many young boxers. Following discussions, Freddie's father signed a contract with Jack's brother Bob, for Freddie to fight George Hasket, another local lad, the following week at Weymouth.

By this time Mr Mills had accepted that nothing would deter his son from becoming a fighter. To try and discourage him would be akin to trying to dam the Thames with a matchbox.

That week, Freddie trained as if preparing for a world championship. Finishing his dairy round by two in the afternoon, he'd sleep until five when his brother arrived home from work to spar with him. After six or seven rounds, he'd skip, shadow-box and do groundwork until Charlie ordered him to stop, warning of the dangers of 'leaving the fight in the gym'. With his mornings spent running behind the float, Freddie couldn't have been in better condition.

Naturally, he was terribly nervous on the evening of his first professional contest. Years later he told me with a grin: 'My knees were actually knocking as I sat in the dressing-room having my hands done.' Yet looking at him any casual spectator would not have believed he was anything but superbly confident. He was fortunate in having Jack Turner's brother, Bob, as his manager. Bob was a calming influence with a lifetime of boxing lore behind him.

Hasket was far more experienced than the Parkstone lad, so that Freddie was not disappointed when the referee declared the contest a draw. In the dressing-room after the fight, Jack Turner handed him eighteen shillings and sixpence. Freddie was earning a pound a week at that time for his milk-round and it seemed to the young boxer extraordinary that he should be paid so much for doing what he enjoyed. His enthusiasm was somewhat modified when he discovered there were deductions to be made. His second took three shillings. The whip, who'd done little more than poke his head round the door to shout, 'You're on now,' took two shillings. And Bob Turner took his thirty per cent manager's commission. By the time he'd settled his debts Freddie had only seven shillings remaining to take proudly home to his mother.

Freddie Mills was now popular with the local boxing fans. His non-stop fighting and readiness to take a punch if by doing so he could get within range of his opponent to unleash his own punches, appealed to them immensely. He was also extremely popular with the local promoters who soon came to appreciate that his name on their bills meant selling seats. Besides which, Freddie never argued about terms. If a boxer pulled out of a contest at the last moment, Mills would immediately offer to take his place without asking 'How much?' or 'What's his weight?'

His second professional contest, which also ended in a draw, was against Stan Nelson. He won his next eight contests by knock-outs, and these included a return with Nelson. Throughout his career, if Mills were beaten or held to a draw, he seldom failed to win the return.

Those vultures of boxing, the managers, scented that Mills was a good investment and took the trouble to point out to his father that at this stage of his son's career the boy must be wisely guided if he were to fulfil his potential. The rag-and-bone merchant was flattered by their attention and, with an engaging simplicity, kept recommending to his son that they should sign with whichever manager had been the last to advise them. Freddie Mills, even at that early age, seems to have been loyal: Bob Turner had looked after him from his first contest and the young fighter refused to sign a contract with anyone else. It is probable that Mills might have reached the top more quickly if he'd signed with one of the big managers like Sam Burns, who, as well as holding a licence, had the advantage of having been Jack Solomons' office manager, or with Harry-the-Horse Levene, dapper Benny Huntman or the ponderous 'Bishop' Jim Wicks.

Bob Turner wasn't a big-time operator but he had close connections with the proprietors of several boxing booths, which were in those days the nurseries of boxers. One of these was Sam McKeown, a West Country operator who was unique in one respect: he insisted on taking ten per cent of any 'nobbins' (coins thrown into the ring by an appreciative audience) earned by his boxers. By the time he was eighteen, Freddie was on McKeown's team.

Today very few boxing-booths survive, maybe because nowadays the BBBC only has 1,000-odd licensed boxers, spread over fourteen weights, whereas in the immediate post-war years there were many more professional fighters spread over eight weights. In this decade any reasonably competent boxer with a good manager can fight regularly at official tournaments; he needn't attach himself to a booth where the pay will be poor and the risks high.

With the spread of television, the public's taste has become more sophisticated and more demanding. The tinsel of fairgrounds is no longer as appealing. More money is around, and the boxing-fan can afford a seat at a tournament, he doesn't need to queue up in a fairground to watch fixed contests. However the dearth of boxing-booths contributes to unskilled boxers' being rushed into championship contests when they are still really learners. In the booths the boxer learned his trade. The young Freddie Mills in McKeown's booth faced fighters two or three stone heavier than himself. He faced tall, rangy men, shorter bull-dog types, clever boxers and farm-boy swingers who could connect with even an experienced fighter if the professional allowed his concentration to wander.

In the booth, the boxers would line up outside the tent, often jogging to keep out the cold. Jack Turner was the spieler who would build up his fighters and gather a crowd. When he had a sufficient audience, he'd announce: 'If any one of you fancies your chance against any of our champions . . . step forward.' He'd pull out a large wad of notes from his inside pocket and count out five. Then he'd look straight at any likely lad: 'If you last three rounds . . . only three rounds . . . just six minutes, that is all . . . these five notes are yours. Who wants to win a fiver? Come and show your girl what you're made of.'

In those days there was a vast gulf between a first-class amateur and a second-rate professional. Today the difference is far narrower because our top-ranking amateurs are really semi-professionals, having already signed contracts with managers before they've won area championships, let alone an ABA title. In fact, the modern manager will often insist his boy remain an amateur until he considers the moment is right for his purpose: maybe the existing champion is getting old, and soon the title will be open. The manager will argue that he would prefer the other contenders to sort themselves out before his boy enters the lists.

In the booth, the amateur challenger had only a remote chance against the professional. But most young men are afraid to admit cowardice and when urged on by their friends some would enter the ring.

In all-in wrestling, there is a traditional format: the villain throws the handsome hero all over the ring until, apparently on the verge of unconsciousness, the hero with his dying gasp pins the villain to the canvas. There used to be a similar pattern in boxing-booths. The professional would appear out-classed, only the expert being able to detect that none of the challenger's punches was actually landing. Then, with only half a minute of the last round remaining, the professional would lash out wildly and appear amazed when the punch landed and his opponent was counted out. All his friends would reassure the challenger that he had been very unlucky, and after a time he might even convince himself it was true.

This was a standard procedure. Inevitably, however, there could be mishaps. Freddie Mills once accepted the challenge of a burly, tow-haired farm labourer. The farmboy was completely unskilled, but years of ploughing and ditching had broadened his shoulders and strengthened his muscles. Without any nicety of style he tore into attack, undeterred by Mills's well-directed counter-punches. Mills thought, of course, that he could land whenever he wanted. Having given the impression that he was about to be beaten, he suddenly stood his ground and set himself for a big punch. Out of the corner of his eye he could see Jack Turner worrying at the danger to his £5. He threw as hard a punch as he was ever to deliver in a championship match, but he might just as well have hit the farmer's boy with a fly-whisk for all the effect it had. The last bell sounded. Jack Turner with an ill grace handed the money over. When the promoter gave Freddie his pay that week, it was £5 short. He said: 'Of course, I'm only taking it off for your own good, to teach you a lesson.'

Years later whenever Mills was asked which was his hardest contest, he'd say: 'Of course, there was that first championship contest with Gus, but actually that was my *second* hardest. Let me tell you about my farm boy . . . bloody great arms like hams.'

If the crowd round the booth failed to be lured into the tent by Turner's spiel, more dramatic methods were necessary. A professional fighter would mix with the crowd and join the jeerers. He would pick on one of his mates lining up outside the tent; gradually the insults would get out of hand, and there would be an apparently vicious exchange of blows before they were pulled apart. Jack Turner would make an impassioned appeal for quiet, and then he'd shout: 'Gentlemen, gentlemen! Come up here and settle your differences in the British way.' The crowd would invariably raise a cheer at the mention of the 'British' way, there being few people more xenophobic than fight-fans. In a few seconds a long queue would be waiting to get into the tent and grab the best seats.

Jack Turner would be smiling again.

Once Freddie was cast as the 'gee-er'. He had bought himself a new suit only the day before. Bill Hood, a close friend, was the professional boxer in the well-worn script. Freddie, who always enjoyed playing the fool, shouted out: 'I could murder that bum with my hands behind my back!' On cue, Hood took a swinger at Freddie. Unfortunately the ground was slippery, as it had been raining, and Freddie fell into the mud. Forgetting his part, Freddie shouted out in fury: 'Bugger it all, Bill. You've fucked up my new suit!'

Bill Hood knew how swiftly a crowd's reaction can shift from humour to anger, especially if they suspect they are being fooled. So as Freddie climbed to his feet brushing the mud off his suit, Hood hit him hard on the nose, bringing a spurt of blood to add to the mud. Mills's reaction was predictable – most good punches are the product of highly developed reflexes. A right hook spread-eagled Hood. The sight of the unconscious Hood and the bloodstained Freddie was enough to convince the most cynical of spectators.

Although Mills was fighting every day in the booth but Sundays, Sam McKeown was always prepared to release him to box in an official BBBC tournament. It was no act of philanthropy: Mills's run of wins was attracting the attention of the sporting press and publicity reacted favourably on the booth. But it wasn't only the local press that was beginning to know the name Freddie Mills. In Klein's Gymnasium, a sordid basement in Fitzroy Square, managers and matchmakers were already mentioning him as a country lad who was knocking out their best fighters.

After his eight knock-outs in a run, Mills suffered his first defeat at the fists of George Davis of Notting Hill. Losing for the first time is a bitter pill for a young fighter. The contest was even up to the last round when Davis landed a hard right to the body. Mills heard the referee counting ten over him but couldn't force his legs to move.

Back in the dressing-room, he was inconsolable. His dream world had collapsed. Fortunately he was given little time for brooding, as he was back fighting in the booth the following afternoon.

George Davis was also being talked about as a future champion, but it wasn't to be. During the war he was killed in a barrack-room accident when a companion was cleaning his rifle.

With Mills defeated for the first time, a return match meant a full house. Davis won again, but this time on points.

The best-known fighter in the booth was undoubtedly Gypsy Daniels, a former heavyweight champion from Wales who was now approaching the end of his career. Daniels had been badly affected by all the blows he'd taken over the years, and as a result most of those who worked at the booth treated him as if he were simple.

The booth boxers were paid fifty shillings a week but augmented their wages with the 'nobbins' thrown into the ring in appreciation of a particularly brave performance, or collected in pails from those at the back of the tent. When he wasn't fighting, Mills enjoyed collecting the nobbins in pails because it gave him the chance to backchat with the crowd. Gradually it became the practice for him to look after one side of the tent whilst the Gypsy looked after the other. Afterwards, in the caravan which McKeown used as his office, Mills was repeatedly surprised to find that though he had collected as many silver coins as copper, the Gypsy's pail only held pennies. Mills at first assumed this was because of the Gypsy's fame: perhaps the punters didn't like appearing to cross his palm with silver. But even when they changed sides, the result was the same: Mills's pail was full of silver and copper, the Gypsy's only of pennies. Even then Mills did not suspect his partner – who appeared so simple – of double-dealing, until the evening he brushed against the Gypsy's dressing-gown hanging on a hook at the back of the caravan door. There was a revealing tinkle. Mills investigated and the mystery was solved. The Gypsy was putting the silver into a pocket, not handing it over to be counted and shared.

It was in the booth and not in an official bout that Mills had his nose broken and received a cauliflower ear. Although the professional booth boxers were much more skilled than their challengers, it was quite impossible for them to avoid all the punches, since they would have ten or more fights, six days a week. By the time the hurricane lamps had been doused and the funfair emptied of customers, the boxers were often too exhausted to do anything but crawl under the ring and fall asleep.

One afternoon, there being no challengers, Mills found himself facing the Gypsy who was at least two stone heavier. In the second round a hard left exploded on Mills's left ear. The younger and lighter man immediately held out his glove in surrender. He told me: 'I wasn't going to play the hero . . . the crowd had already had their ration of blood.'

That night, having helped strike the tent, Mills went back to his digs. His ear seemed to be on fire. His landlady had been catering for booth fighters for many years and had treated a wide variety of injuries. On her advice he bathed his damaged ear in hot milk. But the following morning it was just as painful. Next he applied leeches. Even their insatiable appetites failed to reduce the swelling. From that day until his body was found in the back of his car, he carried the unmistakable hallmark of the professional fighter.

Two weeks later, his nose was broken. Freddie was quite good-looking as a lad, but he was far from upset by the visible damage he'd suffered. Now he was easily recognized by the boxing fans. His enjoyment of being applauded was increasing with every victory.

During his second tour with the booth, he damaged the bones of his right hand – a far more serious injury for a boxer than a broken nose. Jack Turner had seen many boxing careers ended through damaged knuckles. That very evening, to safeguard his investment, he drove Mills across country to Watford to be examined by Eddie Mallet, an osteopath. Mallet was not only an expert bone-manipulator but also promoted boxing at the local town hall. Over the years, because he punched so hard, Mills injured his knuckles several times. He would tell friends: 'If it hadn't been for Eddie Mallet, I'd have had to pack it in.'

In 1937 Mills had twenty-one official contests. He was already facing area champions, but he only lost three: two defeats at the fists of George Davis and a ten-round loss on points to Jack Lewis. The following year he fought sixteen times, winning all but one: a points defeat by the stylish ex-amateur champion Dave McLeave, a meat-porter from Smithfield.

By the start of 1938, Freddie Mills had been widely talked about as a potential champion; now he was being introduced as: 'Our one and only future champion, battling Freddie Mills!'

Nevertheless not all the boxing scribes were convinced of his future success. Gilbert Odd admitted, after Mills had won the world championship, that he had believed Freddie to be too wild and unpredictable to reach the top, and had prophesied that any counter-puncher who stood his ground would beat him.

But a rather more important man in the boxing world did recognize Mills's talent. Jack Solomons, then ruling British boxing, watched Mills fighting at Bournemouth and turning to his companion at the ring-side he remarked: 'There's a future champion . . . and what a crowd-puller!'

But war now interrupted Mills's advance up the boxing ladder. He enlisted, but before he joined the Royal Air Force on New Year's Day 1940, he had one last contest as a civilian, meeting Elfryn Morris of West Bromwich.

Morris was a wily, experienced campaigner, who could adapt his style to discomfit any opponent. He was never afraid to try unorthodox methods. It took Mills five rounds before he began to gain control. The fans at Bournemouth town hall were exchanging glances as if to predict the contest would go the full distance before Mills was declared the winner.

It was between the fifth and sixth rounds that, after a short chat with his second, Morris decided to switch tactics and go on to the attack instead of boxing on the retreat. As soon as the bell sounded for the sixth round, the Midlands fighter was across the ring and within punching distance even before Mills's trainer had slipped the gum shield into his charge's mouth. Mills, sensing his opponent was close, ducked intuitively. Their heads crashed together, and Morris fell to the canvas unconscious. Mills was also out, but he had fallen against the ropes which held him erect. The referee, quite correctly according to the rules, counted out Morris, but, having spread his arms wide to signify that Mills had won, he decided not to try and hold Mills's arm up as the winner. Had he done so, he knew, he might have disturbed the ropes and Mills would have collapsed beside his opponent.

This was the only fight in his career of which Mills hadn't the slightest recollection.

Dr Peter Harvey, consultant neurologist at the Royal Free Hospital, said on my television programme, *The Purse*: 'Every time a boxer is knocked out he suffers brain damage.'

# 5

FREDDIE Mills was called up on New Year's Day 1940 and posted to Padgate in the New Forest. Only two days after reporting for duty he was taken ill and spent a fortnight in hospital with pneumonia. This was the first of several attacks, the last being only a few weeks before his death.

In the early days of the war it was left to regular officers to decide in what capacity the volunteers and conscripts should serve. The officers had little experience of job analysis and few guidelines. Within a few months many jokes were circulating about men and women being posted to jobs remote from their civilian training or capacities. In all three services the appointment officers decided, most illogically, that professional boxers would make ideal physical training instructors. In fact, very few professional boxers are capable of training themselves, let alone their fellow recruits. Boxers are self-centred: their world is that of the gymnasium where they concentrate on their own boxing moves and their own fitness. What others are doing hardly concerns them. They are seldom the types best equipped to instil *esprit de corps* in their fellows.

Mills found that several other well-known professional boxers had preceded him at Padgate, including heavyweight Jack London, flyweight 'banjo-eyed' Peter Kane, Nel Tarleton from Liverpool and his brother-in-law, welterweight Ernie Roderick.

Soon after Mills returned to his unit after sick-leave, he was posted to Uxbridge on a six-week physical training course. Also on the course were Johnny Rust, the South African welterweight who after the war was to become a society hairdresser, and heavyweight Tom Redington who was to become one of Mills's greatest friends.

The course was extremely demanding, both mentally and physically. Mills found that, apart from the usual physical training exercises, he was expected to work out on parallel bars, ceiling bars and vaulting-horses. It was a challenge he didn't relish. He became convinced that he would do himself serious harm and even endanger his boxing career. There seems something a little ridiculous in the mental picture of Freddie Mills, a future world champion, asking for an interview with his commanding officer to plead that the course was too dangerous. Not altogether surprisingly, the CO was angry, but not wanting his irritation to cloud his judgement, he handed the matter over to his sports officer, the international cricketer, R.W.V.Robins. Robins, more amused than cross, pointed out to Mills that during war many men had to risk their lives daily. Indeed, he added, if the war lasted several years an untold number of men and women would never be able to take up their civilian careers again: the dangers weren't particular to professional pugilists. By the time he finished, Mills was ashamed of his complaint and returned to the course.

On the second week of the course, Mills and Redington decided that, though officially they were on duty, they would like to go to the Empire Pool, Wembley to watch the amateur boxing tournament between the United Kingdom and the USA. A batch of recruits was being taken to the famous boxing arena by an RAF coach, and the two concocted an imaginative story to explain why they should join the group, even though they hadn't passes. They need not have troubled, because the sergeant in charge for the evening was former world welterweight champion, Ted Kid Lewis.

Lewis, an amiable if simple man, had attracted considerable animosity in his East End homeland by joining Sir Oswald Mosley's Blackshirts, not realizing that the organization was anti-Semitic. When the truth dawned on him, he paid a visit with his son Morton to Mosley's headquarters, and avenged himself with a couple of right-hand punches which sent the Fascist leader swinging wildly round in his swivel chair. Then, taking his sixteen-year-old son by the hand, he went home, pausing only to stretch flat the two guards on the front door.

Knowing how bitter had been the reaction of the largely Jewish boxing world to his association with the Blackshirts, Lewis was only too anxious to prove he was every boxer's friend. He welcomed Mills and Redington on to the coach and assured them that as long as they were back in good time for the return journey there would be no questions asked. He escorted them personally into the arena so they didn't have to purchase tickets, and stayed with them throughout the tournament, pointing out the celebrities at the ring-side.

'There', he said to the two boxers, 'is the best manager in the country,

Ted Broadribb. What's more,' he added, 'he's straight, which is more than you can say for most of them.'

Mills took only a casual interest in what the East End fighter was saying, his attention being focused on the ring.

Lewis persisted: 'Good fighter too. Beat Georges Carpentier. You couldn't do better, lad, than tie up with him if you get the chance.'

Within months Mills was to recall his words.

At the end of the Uxbridge course, Mills put up his corporal's stripes and was posted to Netheravon. Although he was now a qualified physical training instructor, Mills had no difficulty in obtaining time off to fight. Most senior officers basked in the reflected glory of having boxing stars under their command. Allowing a boxer time off to fight meant that the CO could play host to his senior fellow officers who would, no doubt, be impressed by his close relationship with the star NCO topping the bill.

When Bob Turner telephoned Mills to say he had been offered a contest at Eastbourne against Ginger Sadd, the CO not only gave Mills the evening off but allowed him time off duties so he could train. Two coaches of officers and men travelled with Mills to see him beat the Eastern Area champion on points. His win received national publicity, and his CO promptly suggested that he should form and train a station boxing team at Netheravon. This gave Mills the ideal excuse for avoiding parades and all routine duties. He accepted gratefully.

In these circumstances, he was in no position to refuse when asked to represent the RAF against the Royal Navy. Arriving at Chatham, he learned that his opponent was a middle-rated amateur. (The best amateur would only be a match for a third-rate professional.) Mills was extremely embarrassed.

In the dressing-room, his amateur opponent nervously asked him if he were *the* Freddie Mills. When Mills confirmed this, the Navy man shook his head ruefully. 'Me fight you! I'm only a ham-and-eggs amateur.'

Mills put his arm round his opponent's shoulders. 'Don't you worry. It'll be OK, so long as you take it easy.'

And it was OK – for Mills. No doubt he fully intended carrying his opponent, but as soon as he heard the crowd shouting for him, he forgot all his intentions and cut loose, knocking him out. This victory was one he didn't like to recall.

His next contest was at Walthamstow against the Jamaican light-heavyweight champion, Stafford 'Buzz' Barton, whom he stopped in seven rounds. Two months later he fought before his own people at Bournemouth. He needed all their support, for in the other corner was the heavy-punching, enormously tough Fiji Islander, Ben Valentine. Valentine was so devoid of nerves that he'd fall asleep in the dressing-room while waiting for the whip to call him into the ring. I once asked him how he managed to remain so unperturbed. 'Tony,' he said, 'I was brought up fighting sharks with a small knife to entertain ships' passengers. Why should I have any fear for men in boxing gloves?'

The decision might have gone either way, for Valentine was hitting Mills as hard and as often as Mills was hitting him, but when the Fijian sustained a badly cut eye the referee had to intervene.

Back at Netheravon Mills found himself the local hero. After each of his contests the commanding officer would send for him and demand a running commentary on the fight as seen from the winner's point of view. So when he was summoned one morning to the CO's office he suffered no fears. The CO had been telephoned by Jack Solomons personally to ask him if he would release Mills to fight the British middleweight champion, Jock McAvoy, the Rochdale Thunderbolt. The purse was only fifty pounds, but if Mills won, or indeed gave McAvoy a close fight, he would have broken into big-time boxing.

Fortunately the match was made well over the middleweight limit, since both men, unable to give full time to training because of wartime duties, were well above their best fighting weights. It was a non-stop, all-action contest, neither man giving ground unless forced to do so. By the start of the last round Mills had punched himself out and was on the verge of collapsing from exhaustion. 'I could hardly raise my hands, let alone a gallop. McAvoy was the greatest of gentlemen. He realized I was sold out. "Come on, youngster," he whispered to me in a clinch. "Keep punching. You can do it."'

McAvoy, a great sportsman and puncher, ended his days in an invalid chair.

Mills won three more contests before KO'ing Jack Powell at Reading. Ted Broadribb, at the ring-side, told his companion: 'That lad's got a good left and can take a punch. I fancy him as a future champion.' Broadribb knew that Mills was managed by Bob Turner who was, in Broadribb's world, a small-timer. He reasoned that if he took over the contract it would be of considerable benefit to Mills . . . and himself. He was also at the ring-side for Mills's next fight against Tom Redington, and saw how Mills handled the Manchester heavyweight. The big money was – and is – in the heavyweight division. Mills could never be built up into a full-size heavyweight, but Broadribb didn't see why he shouldn't handle the Goliaths of the ring.

Two days later Broadribb drove to Netheravon and after enlisting the support of Mills's CO, interviewed the young airman. Mills listened to what the manager had to say but remained adamant: Turner had treated him fairly, and he had a contract with him until the end of the year. He insisted on fulfilling that contract. When pressured by Broadribb, he eventually agreed to discuss the matter with Turner.

Bob Turner by now looked on Freddie Mills as his son. He wanted the best for him and knew that Broadribb was in the top echelon of boxing. Furthermore, Turner intended enlisting in the services himself. They therefore reached an agreement that he would remain the nominal manager until the contract expired, but that Broadribb would take over all boxing negotiations, and the two would split the usual manager's percentage of the purses.

Mills's first contest under the new arrangement ended disastrously when he was disqualified for hitting low against Jack Hyams. (Jack 'Froggy' Hyams was so vain, that once when I was sparring with him, I saw he was wearing a hairnet.) Broadribb, undeterred by the disqualification, arranged a fight for Mills at that Mecca of British boxing, the Royal Albert Hall. It was the first time Broadribb had matched Mills against a full-size heavyweight: it wasn't to be the last.

After stopping Tommy Martin, Mills was next in the ring facing giant Jim Wild who outweighed him by over three stone. Then it was Jack London, another Goliath, who was amongst the most resilient and hardest punchers of his day. Chrissie Mills, who was Broadribb's daughter, saw Mills outpoint the West Hartlepool busman: it was the only occasion on which she attended a contest in which her husband-to-be took part.

After defeating Tom Redington again, Mills was matched in an eliminating contest for Len Harvey's crown against Jock McAvoy. The contest ended dramatically, if unsatisfactorily, when the Rochdale fighter tore a muscle in his back in the very first round and had to retire.

Although he now had his three stripes, Mills was becoming increasingly worried by the manner in which his service duties were preventing his training properly. One might have thought that during a war a man's service would take precedence over his civilian occupation, but Mills knew that a boxer's life has a limited span. He handed in his PT badge but was allowed to retain his stripes.

However, there was nothing for him to do any longer at Netheravon and he was posted to South Whitham. There he soon persuaded his new CO to allow him to hang up a punch-bag in the canteen. His roadwork was done on the Great North Road. Having an indulgent commanding officer, he was allowed – as the date of his challenge to Len Harvey grew nearer – to finish off his training at a boxing public house, the Airman, in Feltham.

The championship fight took place in the open air at the Tottenham Hotspur football ground in North London. I was the BBBC inspector for the contest. Mills won the British title by knocking out Len Harvey in the second round, punching him through the ropes and scattering ring-side reporters, who prevented Harvey's falling to the ground. Failing to crawl back into the ring inside ten seconds, he had the first KO recorded against his name in a long and distinguished career which had seen him fight at every weight from fly to heavy.

When he was my inter-round commentator on ITV I once remarked: 'What a dreadful pity you had that KO at the very end of your career.'

Harvey laughed. 'Pity! I got four thousand quid for it. That isn't a bad plaster on a small wound.' He then confirmed what I'd detected from the ring-side: 'I wasn't all that fit. I'd been living it up as an officer in the RAF, I'd been drinking too much and having far too good a time . . . So I thought, "What the hell . . ." And took the fight.'

For a fortnight Mills was on top of the world. He was now British champion with prospects of being matched for a world crown. He would undoubtedly make a great deal of money in the near future. He was content in the RAF with duties which left him plenty of time for training.

Then depression descended on him: he became terse and withdrawn. He said later: 'It was the worst depression I've ever had. I couldn't throw it off. I couldn't face myself, let alone anyone else. It was like a great purple cloud hanging over me.'

He had leave owing to him, but didn't wait for it and instead, going AWOL, ran away to London. 'Afterwards, I couldn't remember exactly what I'd done. I know I went sightseeing. I went to the Tower of London and Madame Tussaud's. As for the rest, I just can't remember. But gradually my senses seemed to creep back.' Returning to his unit, he was unable to explain to his CO what had happened.

Mills's ensuing fits of depression were always hidden from the public who were only allowed to see the outer mask. As a child he'd shown no symptom of mental instability or illness; as an adolescent he had appeared to enjoy life to the full. Was it possible that he was feeling the effects of the punches he had taken?

Once Mills had won the championship, Broadribb saw no reason why he shouldn't follow the big money and have his boy fight the leading heavyweights. Two more victories over Tom Redington and a TKO over Canadian Al Delaney were followed by a return against Jack London. This time the West Hartlepool fighter was much fitter: Mills's best punches had no effect and he was beaten on points.

He returned to winning when he stopped the Scottish heavyweight champion Ken Shaw, who outweighed him by a stone and a half. In this contest Mills showed his chivalry by refusing to administer the *coup de grâce* when the Scotsman suffered a horrendous cut which severed his upper lip.

That was Mills's last contest in 1945, for he was now posted to India. There he saw little of normal service life for he joined a group of leading sportsmen who toured the continent entertaining bored service personnel at air stations and camps. After giving an exhibition he'd answer questions on sport generally. One of his regular companions was footballer and cricketer Denis Compton, who became a close friend.

Returning to England in March 1946, Mills found that he had been matched for the world's lightheavyweight championship against the holder, the American Gus Lesnevich. The fight was scheduled for May at the Harringay arena.

Mills weighed over thirteen stone when he landed in England, and had to train energetically to shed the extra pounds to make the cruiserweight limit. As the inspector for the contest, I examined his bandages at Harringay for the big fight. He showed no signs of nerves, except keeping up a non-stop barrage of badinage with his trainer, Nat Seller.

After an even first round, Lesnevich floored Mills four times in the second with vicious straight rights.

Mills said later that he had no memory of the next six rounds but regained his senses at the start of the ninth when his left hooks began marking the American's eyebrows. At the bell for the tenth round he tore into the attack. Lesnevich measured him with his left and then crashed in a right, which he afterwards claimed to be the hardest punch he'd ever thrown.

I recall sitting with Mills one night years later in Murray's Club as he described what happened afterwards. 'No boxer can hope to be the same after taking a battering like I took that night,' he said. 'Punching like that really shakes up the brain. For a week afterwards I couldn't speak clearly. I slept as if I was in coma, waking up exhausted. Every day I had the most dreadful headaches.'

Despite the hammering he had taken, Mills was not given long to recuperate. Broadribb had been so confident that his charge would win that even before the bout he'd contracted for Mills to fight the British heavyweight champion, Bruce Woodcock. The tickets had been printed and the bills posted. Any cancellation would have cost Solomons money so Mills was forced to go through with the fight. Woodcock won comprehensively on points.

This time even Ted Broadribb thought that Mills should have a holiday. Solomons agreed and took both of them to the USA with him. There Mills met many of the leading boxing characters of the time, including Jack Dempsey, who had a restaurant in New York, and 'Two-Ton' Tony Galento, whose catchphrase was 'I'll moider dat bum!' Mills was at the ring-side for the Joe Louis v. Billy Conn heavyweight championship contest, and was childishly excited to be introduced to George Raft, Frank Sinatra, Pat O'Brien and Tyrone Power.

Broadribb had planned on their staying in the States for several weeks, but after his initial excitement Mills began to suffer bouts of depression and homesickness. They flew back to England within twenty-four hours of Mills telling his manager of his unhappiness.

He wasn't allowed to remain inactive for long. His first contest back at home was short: he KO'd the Swedish heavyweight champion Jon Nilsson in the first round.

There have been many mismatches over the post-war years for which the BBBC must accept some responsibility. It raised no objection when Mills was now matched against Joe Baksi, a Pennsylvanian giant who had not only trounced Bruce Woodcock but broken his jaw in the process. Mills was outweighed by over three and a half stone against one of the most experienced and hardest punching behemoths in the world. He was beaten, bruised and humiliated, his punches having no noticeable effect on the massive ex-miner. Forced to retire, he was afterwards taken to King's College Hospital for treatment to multiple cuts to his eyes. It had been no contest.

# 6

'IN 1947, I shall only fight cruiserweights.' This was Mills's reported New Year resolution. But even before the printer's ink had stained the readers' fingers, Mills was contracted to fight three weeks later at the Royal Albert Hall. Solomons hadn't yet decided who should be in the opposite corner, but Ted Broadribb agreed terms without stipulating anything about the unknown opponent's weight, even though only days earlier the manager had confirmed his boxer's New Year announcement, telling the press: 'In future, my lad will only fight at his natural weight. No more overweight matches.'

This sounded sensible, but had Broadribb stuck to his commitment they would have been out of work, for there wasn't a cruiserweight in the United Kingdom capable of extending Mills, let alone beating him. But the Albert Hall had been booked and a suitable opponent had to be found. Solomons considered the champions of Belgium and Sweden before settling on Willie Quentenmeyer, a Dutchman, and announcing that the contest would be for the European championship. This was a somewhat cavalier statement for Quentenmeyer had already been matched against the Belgian champion for that particular title.

Mills's training for the Quentenmeyer contest was interrupted by a nasty attack of flu, and after the contest he blamed this for his lack-lustre performance. He had suggested that, in fairness to the promoter, he should withdraw from the contest, but Solomons had dissuaded him. 'Even if you are only half fit, Freddie, you'll murder him. The Dutchman isn't in your class.'

Despite being slow and having little experience of fighting Continentals, Mills knocked out his opponent in the second round. But it wasn't a good performance and Mills – always honest with himself – admitted the fans hadn't had their money's worth. The Dutchman should never have been allowed in the same ring as the British lightheavyweight champion.

But although Mills's supporters had been disappointed, they still rallied round him when he opened a Chinese restaurant with his old friend Andy Ho. The Freddie Mills Chinese Restaurant had its front entrance downstairs from 143 Charing Cross Road; the back entrance was into Goslett Yard.

Mills's first contest after the opening of his restaurant was against Enrico Bertoli, the Italian champion, although an American, Lloyd Marshall, had also been suggested. Although he was matched against the world contender, the Italian was confident. Not the least overawed, he took the initiative from the first bell. As usual, Mills had left his stool intent on carrying the fight to his opponent. Bertoli didn't back away but met Mills's hooks and swings with straight jabs which jerked Mills's head backwards again and again. By the fourth round, the Italian was well on top, and trapping Mills in his – Mills's – corner, he threw a barrage of punches to the body. In the past, his opponents had wilted under such punishment. But Mills had an extraordinary ability to take a punch. Instead of sagging to the canvas, he shook that tousled head, spread his feet and began to punch back. A left hook landed flush on the Italian's jaw so that he fell forward. Before his knees could touch the canvas, Mills ripped in a vicious upper-cut. The referee had counted to six when the bell rang.

The minute's rest wasn't long enough for the Italian to recover and he was knocked out within seconds of the fifth round.

Mills's close contest against Gus Lesnevich had made headlines in the USA and Ted Broadribb received several substantial offers for a return to take place in the States. However Lesnevich said no to a defence against Mills in the States, having been impressed by his treatment in the UK. Although he had beaten our challenger, the fans had been generous in their applause for a master craftsman. After dispatching another world challenger, Lesnevich cut short the newspaper debates by announcing that his next contest would be against Freddie Mills for English promoter Jack Solomons.

But by this time Mills and Broadribb had apparently forgotten their words of wisdom earlier and when it was announced that Bruce Woodcock was ill and had had to withdraw from a contest with Stefan Olek, a Polish-born French heavyweight, they immediately offered their services, Broadribb claiming the offer was aimed at helping Solomons out of a difficulty. He used his generosity to increase their share of the purse.

As far as Mills was concerned it all seemed to fall neatly into place: first the contest with Olek, which he was bound to win; then perhaps a second warm-up fight with a leading lightheavyweight, probably Lloyd Marshall; and after that the 'big one' – a world championship return with Gus Lesnevich. But 'The best laid schemes o' mice an' men gang aft a-gley.'

Whilst the press were assessing the odds on each of the proposed contests, Lesnevich had been reconsidering his position and changing his mind. Now the champion told the sports writers that his next defence would be in the States, after all. Solomons, furious at what he saw as double-dealing, told everyone who would listen that *he* would never act in such a manner: he was always straight and expected everyone to act likewise. As far as he was concerned the Lesnevich v. Mills contest was off and instead he would match Mills with Marshall. (The match had already been made, but Solomons shrewdly presented it as an even more exciting project now that Lesnevich – as far as Solomons was concerned – was suspended.)

Mills shrugged his shoulders and started to train with Marshall in mind. Broadribb, however, was of a more devious nature and had already opened secret negotiations with the Transvaal Sporting Club. The result was that Mills was told, to his surprise, that instead of meeting Marshall he would be travelling to South Africa to fight lightheavyweight Johnny Ralph. Both Lloyd Marshall and Stefan Olek had started training to face Mills, but their individual interests could not be allowed to stand in the way of a big purse. The traditional handshake carries little weight in the boxing industry.

Mills and Broadribb flew out to South Africa, accompanied by Don McCorkindale, the South African heavyweight champion. McCorkindale was married to Chrissie, Broadribb's daughter, though by this time their marriage was on the rocks. Nevertheless, father, daughter and son-in-law remained on good terms. Mills liked McCorkindale and a strange friendship developed. When, after the divorce, Mills married Chrissie, McCorkindale spent part of their honeymoon with the happy couple. This raised many rumours. Was there a homosexual relationship between the two men? Was Mills uninterested in sex with Chrissie? Whatever the answer, Mills more or less adopted Chrissie and Don's son, Don junior, who was to be called to give evidence at the inquest into Mills's death.

In later years, Mills always spoke with great appreciation of the days he spent in South Africa. When the contest with Ralph was postponed, far from being irritated, he took the opportunity of travelling.

In South Africa sport is a religion. Wherever Mills went he was acclaimed and surrounded by well-wishers. Once again he showed that he would accept as a genuine friend anyone who told him what he wanted to hear. Although he gave generously of his time, and was always signing autographs, he had one reservation: he couldn't stand being mauled. If anyone put an arm around his shoulders, he flinched away. He would readily stand whilst a queue of autograph hunters formed, but if one of them grabbed him by the lapel of his suit, he would wrench himself free and turn away.

The postponement of the Ralph contest was owing to an injury to the South African's knuckles in training. The damage didn't respond to treatment and for a time it seemed that Mills would have to return home without fighting. The promoter now proposed that Mills should meet Nick Wolmarans, the South African lightheavyweight champion, in the open air. Terms were agreed. Mills stepped up his training. Twenty-four hours before the contest was scheduled to take place the rain pelted down and there was yet another postponement.

In London, Jack Solomons followed the reports of the postponements with apprehension because they endangered his plans, and his pocket. He had wanted to match Mills against Marshall in the open air in Derby week, when sportsmen from all over the world would be converging on London. This was now only six weeks away. If there were another postponement in South Africa, he would have to reimburse Marshall and pay a penalty clause. He cabled Broadribb to fly home.

There *was* another postponement but this was only for twenty-four hours, again because of rain. Mills knocked out Wolmarans in the fifth round and flew home the following day.

Back in England, Mills had only four weeks to prepare for Lloyd Marshall. But there were other demands on his time and concentration. When training, a boxer must focus every thought and all his attention on his forthcoming contest, and Mills, with his unbridled enthusiasm for his trade, had never had any difficulty in doing so. Now he had a new restaurant which he believed, probably erroneously, needed his personal attention. It was a new plaything and there had always been an element of the small boy in his character.

In the evenings after training Mills would play the host at the Charing Cross restaurant, glad-handing old friends and introducing himself to casual guests. There was always a photographer on hand to record him with celebrities. Quickly Mills convinced himself that the success or failure of the Freddie Mills Chinese Restaurant depended upon *his* being there. His training camp took second place. When asked by a newsman about his chances in the fight, he told them: 'Lloyd's been on the planet long enough to qualify for the classification "fistic antique". But the Yanks say he's "old and good".' Neither Mills nor his manager took Lloyd Marshall very seriously.

Meanwhile Bruce Woodcock had suffered the most disastrous defeat of his career at the ham-like fists of ex-miner Joe Baksi. He needed many months of sympathetic support and a most dubious victory before he would regain his confidence. The victim chosen to restore his self-esteem was the American fighter Lee Oma. Oma was a skilled, experienced, ageing boxer, who had no future and came over here solely to pick up the purse. I was in his corner. It proved to be a farce rather than the tragedy it could have been. Every time the American feinted, suggesting that he was going to throw a punch, Woodcock flinched away. It seemed as if the Englishman's hands were lashed to his chest by invisible cords. By the fourth round, Lee Oma hadn't been hit but was running out of breath. 'If he doesn't hit me soon, I'll fall down,' he told us between rounds. At last Woodcock, his head turned away, led with a light left which landed on Oma's shoulder. The American crashed to the floor and was counted out. When Jack Solomons wrote his autobiography, he told how, furious with Oma, he stormed into the loser's dressing-room to find Oma lying on the massage-table with blood dripping from his ear. If blood was dripping, I didn't see it. As we closed the dressing-room door, Oma did a back-flip in the air, and said, 'Back to Murray's Club tonight, eh?' Peter Wilson's column the next day was headlined: *Oma-aroma*!

With Woodcock side-lined, Ted Broadribb saw the chance to add the British heavyweight title to Mills's other crowns. Talking to the press he spoke of the Marshall contest as if it were already behind them. The newspaper experts also wrote as though Mills's victory were inevitable. Their attention was focused instead on a future world-title contest with Lesnevich, who, having eliminated another challenger in the States, was again planning to come to England for his next defence.

Lloyd Marshall was thirty-two. He'd had a long and hard career, he was fast on his feet, knew how to ride a punch, and seldom threw counters unless he was sure they were going to land. It seemed certain that Mills's heavy, non-stop punching would prove too much for him. The press, Broadribb and Mills overlooked the fact that Marshall had beaten four world champions.

Mills was knocked out in the fifth round. Furthermore, he was humiliated.

From the first bell Marshall never looked like losing. Mills, four years younger and ten pounds heavier, was slow, ponderous and appeared almost uninterested in what was going on. Perhaps he had been convinced by the press and his friends that he was invincible and could turn on the heat the moment he wished. Usually a highly trained boxer has a sheen on his skin: Mills's looked pasty and slack.

In the first half-minute, Marshall landed a long, loping, light left. Everyone in the arena saw the punch coming; everyone except Mills. The British champion staggered back, his legs weaving like those of a drunken sailor, his eyes glazed and his gloves hanging down by his knees. Lloyd Marshall didn't follow up. He stood as if he could not credit the result of his punch which had been little more than a tentative swing.

Mills's swaying retreat was halted only by the ropes, where he stood on unsure feet, his guard non-existent. Then slowly – as if waking from a nightmare – he shook his head and turned his face towards Marshall. His legs set wide as though that was the only way they would support him, he waddled forward.

A week later, Mills told the press that after that first punch he was unable to focus and that it seemed to him he was standing at a totally unnatural angle to his black opponent. He saw Marshall, he said, as if the American were contradicting the laws of gravity and was standing in the air at an angle of thirty degrees.

Mills was knocked out resting on one knee, with blood dripping from a cut by his eye. The spectators erupted, shouting: 'Carve up!' 'Rubbish!' and 'Dive!'.

I was sitting at the ring-side close to Mills's corner. Broadribb slammed against my shoulder as he thrust himself to the ring apron, pounding on the canvas with his fist, exploding with fury. A manager should always remain cool and analytical but, in the drama of the fight, he may become so identified with his boxer that he loses all control and gives way to his feelings. Broadribb had shared the plaudits with Mills; now he was sharing his shame. As 'Young Snowball', Broadribb had taken punishment and come back fighting, but his boy, Freddie Mills, had gone down from punches which wouldn't have upset a flyweight.

'Yellow!' he yelled. 'Yellow! Get up, you bastard!' He even spat at his fallen boxer. But by then Mills was beyond hearing.

Later, in the dressing-room, the recriminations continued despite the presence of reporters and officials of the BBBC.

'If you'd taken your job as seriously as you've taken your bloody restaurant, you wouldn't have lost,' Broadribb snarled.

'What the hell do you mean?' Mills, face ashen, was drying his body after a shower.

'Your legs were gone. If you'd done some roadwork instead of poncing about in the restaurant . . .'

Mills looked down at the floor as if seeking enlightenment from the bare boards. 'Rot! I've not been there for a fortnight.'

Broadribb gazed at him with scorn. Then, as if it were not worth challenging the lie, he turned away and strode out into the corridor. A reporter put out his hand to detain him, but Broadribb brushed him aside. 'Anyone can have his contract for peanuts,' he said as he left the hall. Next morning that remark made sporting headlines.

After his retirement, Mills was to write: 'I was panic-stricken, I thought I might have been blinded. So – to put it bluntly – I quit.'

Frank Butler, one of the boxing masters of the press, advised Mills in his *Daily Express* column to 'take a very long rest'. He then asked the pertinent question: 'Have the beatings from Lesnevich, London, Woodcock and Baksi at last taken effect?'

Was Mills aware what was happening after that first punch? Was he suffering amnesia because of its effects on his brain? Peter Wilson of the *Sunday Pictorial* was scathing. 'On two occasions, I think the referee would have been justified in warning Mills for going down from punches which, if they landed at all, should not have had enough to throw him off balance.'

This was a terrible accusation to make against a brave fighter, who had proved his courage again and again. Yet I agreed with every word.

Tonypandy Tommy Farr, the Welsh heavyweight who had killed the legend of the horizontal British heavyweight by his close points defeat by the Sepia Slayer, Joe Louis, was just as bitter: 'Mills should retire before he gets British boxers an even worse reputation than they have . . . and that would be difficult.'

Tommy Farr wrote at the time as if it had been a simple example of lack of guts. Years later a manuscript in Farr's handwriting was discovered and published under the title *Thus Farr*. This autobiographical work shows Farr as a considerably more complex character than he presented to the world. He too found that whilst for one fight one's mood was ready, for another bout the fighter could be beset by doubts and uncertainties. Probably Mills was never able to analyse what really went wrong that night.

When Freddie Mills read the comments of the press and digested the accusations of cowardice, he talked of retirement. In one interview he stated that he wasn't going to be hurried but would think it over for three months before deciding. Naturally all the boxing entrepreneurs and the hangers-on who were used to making money out of Mills found excuses for his dismal display. ('They would, wouldn't they?', as Mandy Rice Davies would have said.) 'If he couldn't see, what else could he do?' 'His mind was numbed, wasn't it?' 'I hear that someone had slipped him a mickey . . .'

But none of the excuses, however dramatic, could account for the fact that Mills could be seen to be out of condition even though he had only recently returned from fighting in South Africa.

Not surprisingly, Ted Broadribb was soon having second thoughts. After all, Mills was his top-earning meal-ticket. Once his anger had abated, his contract with Mills seemed to be worth more than the peanuts he'd mentioned. Surely the fans would turn up at least once more, if only to see whether the champion was really finished?

Boxers have much in common with prima donnas when it comes to backing out of the limelight. A few months away from the ring and the fighter begins to yearn for the scent of wintergreen and the stink of ring-side sweat as the artiste hankers after the smell of greasepaint and the heat of the footlights. Within four weeks of announcing that he would take three months to decide his future, Mills had accepted an offer from Jack Solomons to box the Belgian champion, Pol Goffaux. As an inducement Solomons promised Mills that he would use all his influence to persuade the European Board to make it a championship contest, so that if he won, Mills would hold three titles. Solomons shrewdly appreciated the strength of vanity: Mills signed without demur.

However, the promoter could not be sure that after the Marshall débâcle the fans would pay high prices for seats to watch a beaten man. The tournament needed selling, and at selling Solomons was a master. Each morning the press were fed new stories:

'Mills would train in the Eastern counties. For Marshall he'd trained in London where the air was unclean and he hadn't been able to breathe properly. He was a seaside lad, and needed the countryside to reach his best.'

'Mills banned from his own restaurant.'

'Mills undergoes hypnotism to forget the Marshall fight.'

'Mills determined to make his manager eat his words.'

Because Broadribb had criticized Mills for the time he'd spent in his Chinese restaurant, the fact was emphasized rather than buried: 'Mills ate the wrong food.' It was suggested that because Mills was British through and through, he needed *British* food . . . for this fight he would have English milk, Scottish steaks and Welsh dairy produce.

All this nonsense might have led the more sensitive fan to suspect the public was being taken for a ride and that whatever the result this would be Mills's last contest. To counter this possible reaction, Solomons announced his future plans. After defeating Goffaux, Mills would have a warm-up fight against Ken Shaw of Scotland before challenging Gus Lesnevich for the world lightheavyweight title.

The only logic in the boxing industry is the eventual power of the purse. Contests for championships are seldom between the two best men at the weight. What is far more important than merit when it comes to the big-money fights is whether the contestants are good box-office attractions: not only whether the boxing fans will fill the hall to see them but whether they can ensure television coverage. If a manager or promoter has a champion who is in demand, he will naturally prefer his boy to fight a man who is 'made for him' (that is to say, whom he can beat) than a challenger who might win and eliminate his boxer from the big-time cash.

Mills had been made to look second-rate by an American lightheavyweight who was no longer in the top ten. Yet, according to Jack Solomons, he was only two contests off challenging again for the world title.

Mills hadn't defended his national championship for five years since taking it from Len Harvey. He hadn't avoided challengers but there had been none good enough to have a chance against him, and Solomons hadn't believed the fans would flock to watch Mills bowl over nochancers. But once Marshall's defeat of Mills suggested that the British champion might be past his best, managers of up-and-coming lightheavyweights demanded to know why it was necessary to import unknown Belgians when there were home-grown challengers available.

Broadribb ignored all criticisms. To build up interest in the Goffaux contest, he issued daily bulletins aimed at proving that the Marshall defeat was an inexplicable occurrence and that Mills was now taking his career seriously.

Mills and Pol Goffaux met at the Harringay Arena. Many in the hall must have thought that Mills was his usual confident self as he sat in his corner stool, joking with his handlers whilst the MC made the usual preliminary announcements. However, there is little doubt that as he sat waiting for the referee to call them together, he was hearing in his mind the boos and shouts of 'coward' which had rung in his ears only two months ago.

Certainly, he didn't start in his normal whirlwind style but instead pushed out a couple of weak left jabs which were well out of distance. Then he essayed two long loping left swings that were inches short of the target. In the second round he began to find his rhythm, scoring well with searching straight lefts that opened the Belgian's defence for the following left hooks. In the third round he opened a cut above the Belgian's left eye, and in the following round Goffaux took six counts before retiring.

This victory provided Jack Solomons with the justification he wanted to negotiate a world contest with Lesnevich. There could be few objections to his matching a European, Empire and British champion for the world crown.

Once again challenges flew backwards and forwards. The Luxembourg champion wanted to fight for the European title. Broadribb challenged Woodcock for the heavyweight championship, though even as he posted his challenge to the Board, he must have realized he was courting criticism again for putting his lad into the ring against a fully fledged heavyweight. Anticipating this criticism, Broadribb reasoned that if Mills beat another international heavyweight first, objections to the Woodcock money-spinner would evaporate. Solomons thought similarly, with the result that Mills found himself contracted to face Stefan Olek, a Polish-born Frenchman who had given Woodcock a reasonably close contest.

Mills was in excellent condition for Olek, but at the start of the last round his corner told him that the Frenchman was just edging ahead on points. Mills, at Broadribb's order, began driving an immaculate straight left into his opponent's face, and at the bell he was given the verdict.

1946 had been a disastrous year, with Mills being badly beaten three times. 1947 had been better, in that he had notched four victories against that humiliating defeat by Marshall. Now he was again facing heavyweights . . . and was bound to take punches to his head.

# 7

ALTHOUGH he had only narrowly beaten Olek, the victory was enough to stop any talk of Mills's having to defend his national title against home-grown lightheavyweights. Bruce Woodcock was the only other British fighter at the time who could fill a hall, but Woodcock was injured, so Solomons had either to cancel his next tournament or find a suitable opponent for Mills.

This wasn't easy. Cynics reminded Solomons of what Mills had done to Willie Quentenmeyer. There was even a joke circulating that the Pope would be asked to name the next martyr. The promoter heard the joke and pretended to laugh. He told the press: 'If I can't find the right opponent for Freddie, there'll be no fight. I'm not going to put on a show just for the sake of it – that's not Solomons' way. I've always kept faith with my public . . .'

A few reporters were impressed. Others were suspicious and waited to see what would happen. Their suspicions were justified when the British Boxing Board of Control announced that they were ordering Mills to defend his European championship. Of course, Jack Solomons would fall in with their demands and promote the tournament. The challenger would be the Spanish champion, Paco Bueno. 'Paco who?' asked the fans. 'Paco Pushover!'

The press were bombarded from Solomons' office with hand-outs quoting extracts from the Continental papers listing the Spaniard's wins and extolling his great boxing talent. Eventually, as always, the more gullible began to believe that Bueno stood a remote chance against Mills.

As for Mills, he had signed a contract with Solomons even before the Spaniard's name had been added. But whilst he didn't stipulate whom he would be fighting, there was one aspect over which he felt strongly. For some time the BBBC had been mulling over the possible effects on gates of broadcasting big fights. Many believed that the takings of smaller halls would suffer if the date of the broadcast tournament clashed with their routine shows. Would fans stay at home to listen, or would they remain loyal to watching their sport? The smaller halls are – or were then – the nurseries of boxing, and many promoters barely survived. If the fans stayed away, smaller promoters would go bankrupt and then where would the boxers learn their trade?

Mills wanted his European defence to be broadcast, but the Board vetoed the proposal. Mills's reasons for persisting in his demands were not selfish. He would benefit personally from the broadcast: he'd receive a cut of the BBC fee, small though that might be. But ever since he had served in the RAF he'd taken a keen interest in ex-servicemen's well-being, especially those in hospitals and homes like those of Roehampton and St Dunstan's. He had a host of supporters in these homes and had received many letters emphasizing that if his fights were broadcast the ex-servicemen, many still suffering from war wounds, would be able to cheer him on from their beds. Freddie reacted to their appeal by telling the Board that if the fight were *not* broadcast he would pull out.

The Board was singularly unimpressed by his threat. Charles Donmal, the general secretary, remarked to the press: 'If Mills doesn't fight, he doesn't. That's all.' Broadribb reported this decision to his boxer as Mills worked out at the Windmill Street gymnasium – Mills had started training in earnest, having learned his lesson painfully at the fists of Lloyd Marshall.

Most of the press agreed with the Board. The broadcasting of boxing was inevitable . . . but not yet. When Mills maintained his opposition to the Board's decision, one reporter reminded him that he was a professional fighter and not a social reformer: he should leave campaigning to the press. Mills was hurt by the criticism. But although he was disappointed he realized that to persist would be to go against the popular view . . . and Mills lived for popularity. He told friends: 'I've done all I can. I wanted my supporters in the services and hospitals to be able to hear it. But if the powers that be say "no", then I'll have to accept it.'

Paco Bueno arrived in London four days before the contest, five pounds overweight. Fortunately, he wore a beret, which gave the press something to write about. Funny foreigners were still good copy.

The contest was as big a fiasco as the Goffaux bout had been. After a first round in which both men tested each other's reactions, Mills landed a light left-hook, followed by a short right to the jaw. Bueno promptly crashed to the canvas and remained there motionless till a good minute after the referee had completed the count. The crowd, who had paid high prices for a European championship, had seen four minutes' dancing and two light punches. They booed both boxers every step of the way back to the dressing-rooms.

Boxing followers complained bitterly that they had been taken for a ride by the pre-fight hype and vowed they would never go to another Mills contest unless they knew a great deal more about his opponent. Solomons was shrewd, and the very next afternoon he published a cable, which he claimed to have received that very morning, offering him a fight for Mills against Tami Mauriello, the Italian-American heavyweight, in London. Eighteen months previously, Mauriello had KO'd Bruce Woodcock: no one could suggest that Mauriello was another sacrifice.

Broadribb publicly accepted the proposal, realizing it would take many months before such a fight would be settled and that much could happen in the mean time. Despite past experience, Broadribb was still prepared to put Mills into the ring against heavyweights. Woodcock would be out of the ring for many months through injury: perhaps the Board could be pressured into declaring the title vacant? If so, Freddie Mills would certainly be one of the challengers.

At a dinner in the States given to honour Gus Lesnevich as 'fighter of the year', the lightheavyweight champion had told the guests that he had several contests in view, one of which would be to defend his title against Freddie Mills in London. Broadribb saw that such a match would be a money-spinner, and also a far more attractive possibility than Mauriello, who, at a stone and a half heavier than Mills, had knocked out more than fifty of his opponents and given giant Joe Baksi such a rough handling that the Czech-American had refused a return.

Solomons could always twist facts to suit circumstances. On a radio programme I once asked him if the gold initials S.J. on his tie pin stood for Society of Jesus, so Jesuitical could he become when defending himself. Asked if Mauriello really wasn't too big for Mills, Solomons shrugged his shoulders as if he couldn't understand why such a question should be posed. He had been accused of matching Mills against 'Continental bums'; Mauriello had been beaten by Lesnevich; no one doubted that Mills would be in with a chance against Lesnevich . . . So?

Peter Wilson countered by reminding his readers of Mills's words in his dressing-room after being knocked out by Baksi: 'He was just too big. I'm sticking to lightheavyweights in future.'

Solomons, seeing the warning signs, extricated himself from the Mauriello negotiations, telling the press he had cabled the American with a firm offer but, having received no reply, the contest was off.

Mills's friends sighed with relief.

Before the news of the Mauriello cancellation was in print, the press were told that Mills had been offered a contest with Johnny Ralph in London. Because the South African was still having trouble with injured knuckles, this fight could not take place until May.

All these machinations had taken time and Solomons was forced to cancel his March booking. That cost him money. If Mills was going to fight Ralph in May, there was no reason why he shouldn't be ready for a return with Lesnevich in early summer. That still left April with nothing booked. Woodcock, if recovered, might fight Mills for the heavyweight title? Lloyd Marshall might be tempted to come back to London to give Mills his revenge?

Other promoters resented Solomons' almost total monopoly of the British lightheavyweight champion. One offered Lesnevich £15,000 to come to London and fight Mills on one of *his* promotions. Solomons reacted like a mother whose child is threatened, claiming that he was the only logical promoter for such a contest, having promoted their previous fight. He did not, however, offer Lesnevich's manager, Joe Vella, similar terms to those offered by his rival but cabled him suggesting that the American fought on a percentage basis, and describing the £15,000 offered by his rival as 'crazy'. Joe Vella wasn't so sure and asked for time to consider the idea of a percentage.

Meanwhile, Solomons had his April tournament to fill. He solved that riddle: Mills would fight Ken Shaw in an eliminator for the heavyweight championship. It was all very tidy: Mills v. Shaw in April, Mills v. Ralph in May, Mills v. Lesnevich in July.

Since their last contest, Ken Shaw had grown a moustache to camouflage the deep scar on his mouth resulting from their first encounter. In their second fight, once again Mills demonstrated his gallantry when facing a badly injured opponent. Shaw started the action by sending Mills reeling back on to the ropes with a hard right. Mills countered with a left hook which dropped the Scot. Shaw was up on his feet at the count of two but was immediately put down again from a short right. When he staggered to his feet again he was bleeding badly from his mouth. Mills, realizing that it had been slashed open again, stood back, inviting the referee to stop the contest before the wound worsened. The referee, ignoring Mills's appeal, tersely ordered: 'Box on . . . I'll tell you when to stop.'

Mills looked to his corner. His seconds waved him forward. He paused. But he was a professional.

In all, Shaw took five counts before his seconds threw in the towel. The big Scot spent the night in Charing Cross Hospital having stitches inserted into a wound which spread from the corner of his nose to the side of his mouth.

The Shaw fight gave another insight into Mills's complex character. With most professional boxers the sight of an opponent in deep trouble is enough to unleash the innate aggressiveness which is an essential part of a fighter's make-up. Ted Kid Lewis summed up this reaction: 'When I see he's badly hurt, I throw everything in. Whilst he's there, I hate him. He stands between me and everything I want.'

Mills was a naturally aggressive fighter. He too was ambitious and wanted fame and money. Yet he proved in this fight – as he showed on other occasions – that his sense of compassion was greater than his inborn ferocity. This suggests a sensitivity which might have torn him apart if, as has been suggested, he had been anticipating arrest shortly before his death.

Solomons had now struck a deal for the Mills v. Ralph contest to be staged in South Africa. However, once again Ralph was hurt in training and the fight was postponed. Broadribb decided that he should fly out to find out what exactly was happening and whether they were being given the runaround by the South Africans. Mills stayed at home in South London, living in his manager's home so that he could keep Chrissie company.

There had also been a hitch in the Lesnevich negotiations: because of the financial restrictions operating at the time, the Treasury had threatened to ban Lesnevich taking his share of the purse out of the country. This barrier was now removed.

Although the Ralph fight seemed less and less likely to take place, Mills dared not relax his training, for if he were to have a chance of beating the American he couldn't afford to be anything less than at peak fitness.

Nat Seller, his trainer, thought matters over. It is all too easy to overtrain a fighter. Mills, extremely susceptible to atmosphere, wanted to be surrounded by friends and admirers; he was almost afraid of being alone. Maybe only company could keep his doubts away and still his pre-fight nerves? Now he was faced with several weeks of intense training during which boredom would hang over him like a cloud. Seller finally chose as a training camp the Barley Mow at the foot of Box Hill – close enough for trips to London, but far enough to keep Mills from Chrissie. The landlord, delighted at the free publicity, erected a ring in the garden behind the public house. Mills and his entourage took over.

Every evening in the back room of the bar, Seller and Mills watched the film of his first contest with Lesnevich, analysing Mills's mistakes and Lesnevich's style. What they learned from this would provide their strategy for the return.

The reports to the press from the training camp laid great emphasis on the fact that Mills was paying his sparring partners £2 a round. With wages as high as this they could expect no quarter. The memory of how Mills had skimped training for the Lloyd Marshall fight had to be eclipsed by news that he would never be fitter than he was at the moment. As usual in the weeks and days before a big fight, rumours abounded. It was whispered that Lesnevich was having difficulty making the lightheavy-weight limit. Those 'in the know' related that the American had lost his taste for hard training. Nat Seller, an experienced boxing operator, had heard this kind of rumour before, especially in the States where boxing is even more of a jungle than in Britain. He dismissed the stories as an attempt to lure Mills into over-confidence.

Yet at the weigh-in it seemed that there might be substance to the rumours, for Lesnevich looked pale and drawn. The British sports journalists hoped Mills would win but prophesied a Lesnevich victory.

Teddy Waltham was to referee. He was an ex-welterweight professional boxer who'd topped bills in minor halls as 'Teddy Waltham of Waltham Cross'. In a few years he would be appointed the general secretary of the BBBC. I was one of the two inspectors of the Board chosen to stay with the fighters to see the rules were scrupulously observed.

As Mills sat in his dressing-room having his hands bandaged, I had an excellent opportunity of watching him. I had never seen him so tense. He talked incessantly as if the flow of his words would bring him reassurance. The sentences were frenetic. His eyes flitted from face to face, seeking emotional support from each of us. There could be little doubt that the importance of the occasion was too much for his nerves. I have seen this happen before, with the result that by the time the boxer was in the ring he was totally exhausted and in no condition to give a good performance. Fortunately, at least twenty minutes before Mills was due in the ring, Sid Field, the comedian, came into the dressing-room to wish him luck. At a glance he realized Mills's state of mind, and taking off his coat he put on an act as if he were performing before a full house at the Talk of the Town. The tension seemed to seep out of Mills and by the time Seller wrapped his dressing-gown round his shoulders for the trek to the ring-side, Mills was completely relaxed.

The White City was sold out. Touts in the street outside were flogging five-guinea tickets for anything between £25 and £40.

The strategy devised at Box Hill demanded two tactical moves from Mills. Lesnevich's straight right was classic and could stop any man. Having repeatedly landed it on Mills's jaw in their first encounter, Lesnevich would expect that in the return Mills would circle away from it, so keeping out of distance. If instead Mills attacked from the first bell, using his own right hand, it would take the American by surprise. Whatever the outcome of this ruse, Mills would then concentrate on boxing rather than trying to out-fight and out-box the champion. Lesnevich boxed from an upright stance, using straight punches. He was used to his opponents trying to get past these leads by ducking and weaving, and throwing hooks over the top of his punches. How would he react if his opponent boxed with his own style? Honey Francis, a wise old trainer, used to advise: 'Box a boxer, fight a fighter, punch a puncher . . . they never know what to do then.'

In the corner, Broadribb lectured Mills on the importance of his sticking to their plan whatever happened. Even though Mills nodded his acceptance of the instructions, Broadribb and Seller exchanged glances, wondering whether, when the bell sounded, Mills would revert to his usual style and throw caution to the winds, punching with both hands.

Their first tactic worked better than they could dare have hoped. Within seconds of the bell, a searing right from Mills split the American's left eyebrow. As he staggered back, Mills followed the right with a left hook which opened an old wound over the champion's other eye. Lesnevich returned to his corner with blood streaming down both cheeks.

Mills certainly won the first round. The next three were even. In the fifth, Mills, dangerously growing in confidence, forgot his orders and tried to out-fight Lesnevich. The champion coolly picked Mills off with his long left and easily took the round. In the corner, Broadribb, his face scarlet with rage, shouted: 'Box him . . . box him! You'll win. Fight him and he'll *do* you.'

In the next round, because of his manager's orders, Mills was ultra-cautious and hesitated to attack. Time was of utmost importance to the champion who wanted his seconds to have every possible chance to work on his damaged eyes, and knew that if he and Mills didn't exchange blows there would be more likelihood of the wounds closing. So the champion bided his time and the two circled each other, feinting and moving in and out of distance, without either landing.

The spectators became restless. Those furthest from the ring and remote from the drama began to catcall. Teddy Waltham, sensing the change in the fight, called the boxers to him at the start of the next round and demanded more action. But in the interval Broadribb reiterated his advice: 'Bugger the ref. Fight and you'll lose, box and you'll win.' Seller, his head close to Mills's, added: 'They're working on his eyes. Keep punching them, and you'll stop him.'

So Mills continued to box and Lesnevich stayed out of distance. The catcalls grew louder. Somewhere in the stadium some of the crowd slow-clapped. By the tenth round, Waltham was exasperated. He ordered, 'Stop boxing!' and speaking just loud enough to be heard over the boos, said: 'This isn't like your first fight, fellows! You *must* give more or they'll tear the place apart.'

Mills had never been warned before for not fighting. As soon as they faced each other again, forgetting the orders from his corner he threw a wild left hook to Lesnevich's chin. The sudden change in tactics took the champion by surprise and he failed to block the blow. He was down. The American was on his feet before the referee could pick up the count from the timekeeper, but he was dropped again by another left hook. This time he let the count reach eight before dragging himself upright. Mills, tense with excitement, coiled himself to attack. But before he could throw another punch, the champion crumpled to the canvas again, his eyes vacant under his swollen, bloody brows.

This time Lesnevich had gone down without being hit. According to the rules, the count should have continued. Immediately Broadribb was half-way across the ring to embrace his champion. Teddy Waltham, however, gave no indication that the contest was over, and, instead, hustled Broadribb out of the ring before turning towards Lesnevich again. By now the American, a great and brave champion, was standing up, his right hand cocked as if to dare Mills to come within distance. After the fight, Lesnevich admitted that he was foxing: 'I was out on my feet, and that's the truth,' he said. But the pretence worked. Mills was uncertain what to do. One moment he had been leaping with joy believing the fight finished, and the next he was facing the man who had stopped him the first time they met and was clearly still dangerous. The bell rang and the chance was lost.

The next round Lesnevich used all his skill to avoid trouble, keeping Mills off balance with his left or moving out of distance when threatened. By the twelfth round he had fully recovered and, taking the initiative, notched up points, winning the round. When the bell brought them out of their corners for the last round, there wasn't a great deal between them, though the judges had Mills ahead on account of the knock-downs.

By now the crowd had forgotten their anger at the inactivity of the middle rounds and were yelling for Mills to make a grandstand finish and so put the decision beyond all doubt. The men touched gloves. From then until the final bell they stood toe to toe punching each other to the edge of total exhaustion. When Mills flopped down on to his stool, Nat Seller threw his arms about him, bellowing: 'You've done it, Freddie! You've done it! You're world champion!'

In those days a world champion could earn many thousands of pounds by sponsoring goods and making personal appearances; today it is millions. To get the most out of winning a championship, the boxer usually needs shrewd advisers who will not only look after the cash as it rolls in but will protect the fighter from the vultures. Mills had as counsellors Broadribb and Solomons. Neither was exactly a philanthropist: each knew full well that the title was worth a fortune to him personally. Whilst looking after Mills, they would not forget their own interests. Mills was still young and strong, but there is a limit to every boxer's length of service!

Before the championship contest, it had been suggested that after beating Mills, Lesnevich should fight Joe Louis for the heavyweight title. There is a boxing legend that on one occasion when his boy was taking a terrible hiding a well-known manager had turned to the ring-siders and said: 'Don't worry . . . *we* can take it!' Broadribb now challenged Louis on behalf of Mills. There can be no argument that Mills, a twelve-stone-four-pound fighter, wouldn't have stood a chance against the sixteen-stone Louis, whose fists moved so fast that few of the fighters he knocked out ever saw the punches which finished them. In retrospect, one can only hope – charitably – that it was more an advertising stunt than a sincere proposition.

A champion is seldom short of challenges. It is his prerogative to pick and choose from among his challengers the order in which he will meet them. Johnny Ralph chose this moment to declare himself fit and call on Mills to honour his agreement to fight him in South Africa, the promoters adding another £12,000 to their earlier offer as an inducement. The Madison Square Garden entrepreneurs talked in many thousands about a third championship contest with Lesnevich, this time to be in New York. Another possible contest would be against Bruce Woodcock for the heavyweight title, a fight for which Mills had qualified by beating Ken Shaw.

Broadribb became more and more expansive as he realized the options open to them, suggesting that, before meeting Louis, Mills might have a warm-up contest against Jersey Joe Walcott. Some warm-up contest! Jersey Joe was not only going to win the world title but again was far heavier than the British fighter. Mills's dismal record against heavyweights had been conveniently forgotten. Managers and promoters don't take the punches.

Whom he fought next wasn't solely up to his manager, Ted Broadribb. For all contests at the lightheavyweight limit Mills was already contracted to Jack Solomons. But it wasn't only a legal document which bound Freddie Mills to him: Freddie, a loyal friend, looked upon the promoter as his friend. Solomons had kept faith with him even when he'd suffered that humiliating defeat by Lloyd Marshall; Solomons had given him the chance to re-establish himself. Mills refused to fight Lesnevich in the States unless Solomons agreed.

Pressing for a rubber match between Mills and Lesnevich, Joe Vella reminded Broadribb that the Americans had kept their promise for their champion to defend his title in London. He now expected the Englishmen to behave just as honourably.

Solomons told Vella – and everyone else who would listen – that he'd always been a man of his word. No one could ever accuse Jack Solomons of welshing. Cynics recalled the words of poet Ralph Waldo Emerson: 'The louder he talked of his honour, the faster we counted our spoons.'

Mills could and would be exploited. He was British and we had had few world champions at any weight. Solomons, asking himself whether this 'capital' should be handed over to the Americans, suffered from a convenient amnesia and denied that he'd ever made any promise about a return in the States. Vella, who'd been in the boxing game a long time, wasn't surprised. He now offered Broadribb £37,000 for Mills to defend his title at Madison Square Gardens. Broadribb worked with Solomons, but . . .

Every boxing journalist had his own ideas about whom Mills should fight next. Mills didn't join in the guessing game. At this particular time he didn't want to fight anyone. Although he was now world champion, he had been dissatisfied with his performance against Lesnevich. He told a journalist: 'All through – certainly up to the last two rounds – I missed the boxer's greatest asset: co-ordination. My punches were always behind my intentions.' Other boxers would have kept this self-criticism to themselves; Mills told the world of his doubts. Such modesty could only enhance his popularity. Few friends bothered to ask themselves why he had been lacking co-ordination when he had trained so hard.

Broadribb knew he could use this tale in his negotiations to obtain breathing-space, if it became necessary. So as to have medical evidence for the Board, if needed, he sent Mills to a consultant physician. The doctor recommended that Mills should take a holiday for at least two months.

The Americans, who had a large financial interest in Mills's being fit to fight, interpreted the doctor's recommendation as another move in Solomons' game of bluff and super-bluff. Again they urged that 'gentleman's agreement'. Broadribb rounded on them. 'Freddie has been suffering from headaches and dizziness which grow worse each time he starts training. Frankly, I think he's on the verge of a nervous breakdown. When he's better, we'll talk and take Lesnevich . . . not before.'

Joe Vella didn't believe a word of it and pressed for the Board to fix a date. Broadribb replied that he would rather his fighter retired than fought in his present frame of mind. Intent on persuading the American to offer a still larger purse, he encouraged the Lesnevich backers by telling them: 'Freddie took so much punishment in the second round of their first fight that he was in a daze for the rest of the week.'

Vella persevered. Broadribb sent Mills to see another specialist. It is doubtful whether the manager believed his boxer's complaints about his health, but Mills still insisted to his family, at this period in his life when he had achieved almost everything he had fought for: 'The headaches and dizziness recurred again and again. I was very depressed and very down.'

After the second consultation, Broadribb showed the press an X-ray which he explained showed there was a slight displacement at the base of Mills's spine. With explanations, excuses, accusations of lying and recriminations thundering between the States and the UK, the BBBC ordered Mills to visit their own specialist. With the consultant's report in his hand, Charles Donmall issued a press handout: 'The examination has shown that Mills will not be able to train to take part in his return fight with Gus Lesnevich. Whatever happens, that date will have to be cancelled. Mills's future in the ring has not been definitely decided.'

This statement was vital to Mills. It anticipated any punitive action the American Control Board might make to deprive Mills of his title so that they could stage another version of the world's championship in New York.

At American instigation another X-ray was taken. This time the radiographer opined that the site of the displacement was not at the base of the spine but was, in fact, 'a slight disalignment of the vertebrae at the base of the skull'.

Could this displacement have caused the mental sluggishness and clumsy physical reactions of which Mills had complained?

Mills's ailment was never fully diagnosed or treated. Did the symptoms recur years later, after he had retired, so that Mills suspected he might be suffering from punch-drunkenness? Mills would have seen many old-time fighters hanging about the dressing-rooms earning a few shillings by carrying the bags of up-and-coming fighters – shambling, incoherent shells of men who were reaping what punches received years before had sown. Mills was an intensely proud man. He could never have faced such a future for himself if he believed the punishment he had already taken was catching up on him.

The enforced inaction owing to ill-health had one practical advantage. Mills had earned so much money over the previous taxation year that if he had fought again he would only have received sixpence in the pound of his purse. Despite the shortness of a boxer's career there was no spread-over when it came to income tax.

The stories about Mills's taxation problems, combined with the contradictory reports of the X-rays, added to the Americans' suspicions that Broadribb had decided to avoid a third meeting with Lesnevich by any means. They were further incensed when, within a month of the Board report, yet another medical bulletin was given to the press: 'Mills is having special treatment which is working so effectively that he will probably be back training by November.' They were angry but not surprised by the additional information: 'Before fighting Lesnevich, Mills will have a warming-up contest against Johnny Ralph.'

Mills was now at the height of his popularity in this country, whatever the Americans might think about his refusal to fulfil his contract to them. In the street strangers stopped him to shake his hand. Groups of urchins dogged his footsteps. He was made a Freeman of the City of London on the very day he was married to Chrissie (née Broadribb) McCorkindale at the Herne Hill Methodist Church.

Freddie and Chrissie had decided to keep the wedding secret. Though Mills habitually courted publicity, he considered the ceremony too personal to use as an advertisement. However, one journalist caught a whisper of their plans and during the service he waited outside the church, no doubt congratulating himself on his scoop. Mills, told about the reporter, left by the back door. Mills had many friends in the press and realised that what one knew the others would soon find out. Back at home for the reception, he telephoned all the leading boxing journalists so that within an half an hour the house was thronged with boxing writers and well-wishers.

The honeymoon was short, and three days later Mills began light training for his contest with Johnny Ralph. Five days afterwards he broke training to travel to Bournemouth to receive an illuminated address from the Mayor of his home town. After the ceremony in the Mayor's Parlour he was asked about the proposed fight with Lesnevich and whether he was prepared to cross the Atlantic. His answer killed off any American hopes. 'That's up to Jack Solomons. Jack's always treated me fairly. I wouldn't fight for anyone else unless he agreed to release me.' The idea of Jovial Jack's allowing such a good meal-ticket to fight for anyone else was unthinkable.

Mills flew to South Africa a fortnight before his contest with Ralph. Since he had won the world championship at lightheavyweight, the bookmakers quoted Mills as the three-to-one favourite. This had a damping effect on the sale of tickets. On instructions from the promoters, the press drew the attention of their readers to Mills's very poor record fighting full heavyweights, adding that Ralph had stopped Nick Wolmarans in two rounds fewer than it had taken Mills to do the same. The odds shortened and interest revived. In the mines, where partisanship was most fervid, Ralph was favourite by the time the bell brought the fighters together.

To nurture interest during the week before the fight, Mills appeared nightly on the stage of the local cinema. He shadow-boxed, skipped, answered questions from the audience and displayed his championship belt which he'd been awarded by the *Ring* magazine. It was the first time he had performed on a stage, other than to present prizes or be introduced, and he found the experience exhilarating. He felt excited and yet safe when the audience applauded him: it filled a need. This week at a South African cinema gave him a taste for theatre life which was to decide his career when he finally hung up his gloves.

The fight with Ralph justified the original odds laid by the bookmakers. Ralph narrowly won the first round. Then Mills, having weighed up his opponent, knocked down the South African several times before stopping him in the eighth round.

The week after his victory Mills was on the stage again, this time in Cape Town. Now he had defeated their champion, the South African fans were even more ready to acclaim him. He began to learn how to move naturally on the stage, how to take time with his words so they could reach the back of the hall. Actors and music-hall artists were all eager to help and advise him. This was his apprenticeship for his future.

At the invitation of master batsman Denis Compton, Mills attended an MCC match at Newlands. Trying to call on his host in the dressing-room, he was refused admission as it would have entailed his going through the members' club-room. To the members of the club this was unthinkable . . . after all, Mills was only a professional pugilist. Mills was more amused than angry at the self-importance of the Newlands Club members, especially in view of his enthusiastic welcome everywhere else. However, the sporting press of South Africa were not so forgiving; the following morning the story made headlines, and the comments were extremely critical of the club officials. The president of Newlands Club, attempting to explain their point of view, said: 'I didn't think a prize-fighter would be at home or mix with members of a club like ours.' This did little to mollify the press.

Told of the president's words, Mills shrugged. 'Lucky the City of London didn't think like that or I wouldn't be a Freeman today.'

The anecdote was repeated among cricket enthusiasts and boxing followers, growing in bitterness with the telling. Eventually a mutual friend brought Freddie Mills and the club chairman together. Mills told the chairman how bored he'd become with the story. The following morning, a much-chastened official gave a more helpful interview to the press: 'All misunderstandings have been removed,' he said. 'The chairman has had the pleasure of meeting Mr Mills and wishes to pay tribute to his generous understanding of the situation.'

Mills's reaction was typical of his friendly nature. He was voracious for publicity but had no time for petty vendettas. When friends later mentioned the story, he told them: 'It's all a lot of nonsense. The Newlands members aren't a bad lot of fellows.'

Towards the end of November, Mills returned to London to find Jack Solomons waiting for him at the airport. Solomons wanted to put Mills into another contest within the month. But Mills was tired and needed to wind down after the South African adventure, so whilst Solomons talked as they drove back to London, Mills closed his eyes and didn't answer.

1948 had been a wonderful year. Mills had won the world championship, and been married. He'd moved into a house on Denmark Hill and started a new life as a family man. He was world famous, and the whole sporting fraternity was waiting to know his plans. If anyone had suggested that his fight with Johnny Ralph would be Mills's last victory, the prophet would have found few believers.

# 8

AFTER a few days at home, Mills was impatient and ready to consider his future plans. He had a wide range of challengers. Some of them were feasible opponents, others were too bizarre to merit consideration. Having discarded the impossibles, he and Broadribb weighed up the advantages and disadvantages of each possible match.

One contest appealed to them more than any other. Mills now held four titles, including the world lightheavyweight championship, but Bruce Woodcock was still the holder of the heavyweight crown. Mills had qualified to fight Woodcock by beating Ken Shaw and when he'd met Woodcock before he had only been out-pointed. The public would pay well to watch their two favourites, and Mills believed he could out-box and even out-punch the Doncaster fighter. Rumours were abounding that Woodcock had lost his zest for boxing. Mills, on the other hand, was confident that this time he would be better prepared and stand a good chance.

But before Broadribb could conclude negotiations for a Woodcock bout, they had to await the result of Woodcock's fight against the American, Lee Savold. If Savold defeated Woodcock, the British heavyweight championship would be less of an attraction. Mills might then earn more money by challenging the American, even though no championship would be involved.

Meanwhile in the States, the promoters of the modestly termed Tournament of Champions wanted to include in their bill a world lightheavyweight championship. Anticipating Broadribb's agreement, they announced that a Mills–Lesnevich return would top the bill. Broadribb was furious at their presumption, but his anger cooled when he was told that the impresarios were prepared to pay £20,000. Whether he could accept such an attractive purse offer now depended on Jack Solomons' being prepared to waive his interests.

Solomons, realizing that the British press would roast him if he stood between Mills and such a contest, agreed, but stipulated that the tournament must take place after April by which time Mills would have fought either Woodcock or Savold on his (Solomons') London bill.

Yet another offer was received by transatlantic cable: this time the proposed opponent was Ezzard Charles, and again the money was good. But Broadribb had given his word – Mills would fight in the Tournament of Champions. He welcomed Solomons' intervention, for by April Mills's taxation problems would be simplified, but it meant abandoning the idea of waiting to see whether Woodcock could beat Savold before deciding on Mills's next contest. There were delays. Broadribb told the press: 'Freddie needs a rest. He's not been fit. I'm sure he'll be ready by April, but not before then.' The position was becoming more and more complicated.

The world championship is of financial value not only to the champion and his manager but also to the promoter who stages the fight. At that time, America had almost a monopoly of world champions, and in defeating Lesnevich Mills had deprived the American promoters of one of their best meal-tickets. Given the least excuse, they would have demanded that Mills be stripped of his championship if he didn't defend his title within the allotted time. The championship would then be open and they could stage an eliminating contest before their much advertised tournament. Probably both contenders would be American, which would guarantee that the control of the championship remained with them. Broadribb had to make sure that he gave them no excuse to make any official complaint that Mills was playing for time.

In making sure that Mills was legally forbidden to fight before April, Solomons had anticipated such American machinations. They could hardly apply for a boxer to be stripped of his championship if he were specifically prevented from fighting by a contract with another promoter. If they did, Mills would undoubtedly receive heavy damages in court.

Promoters don't accept being out-manoeuvred without fighting. The Americans countered by appealing not to the world authority but to the BBBC, with whom they enjoyed excellent relations. They urged the Board to insist that Mills defend his world title without delay. The Board were in a difficult position: if they gave way to the Americans they would be bitterly criticized by the entire British press. They therefore played for time, asking Solomons and Broadribb to explain why they were apparently trying to keep the lightheavyweight title in cold storage.

Broadribb appeared before the stewards of the Board, unapologetic.

He agreed with the Americans that he had promised Mills would defend the championship against Lesnevich, but he pointed out that the Americans had taken a long time to offer suitable terms and that, in the mean time, out of fairness to his fighter he had been forced to accept other offers, pointing out that he was contracted for Mills to fight Woodcock for the British heavyweight championship. Mills was the only logical contender. Smiling, he asked: 'Are you suggesting that I withdraw Freddie from the national championship to satisfy Yankee demands?' The Board decided it was safer not to intervene.

Now Mills had to face three months of inactivity. He had already discovered how quickly a boxer can lose the fine edge of his reactions through idleness, and knew how easily muscles can become soft if not exercised daily. He decided to keep in light training even though it wouldn't be practicable to work-out in the gymnasium every day. He erected a lean-to in his garden, which later he incorporated into the house itself, and hung a heavy bag in the shed. Whatever time he'd gone to bed, he worked out early in the morning on the bag as well as running two or three miles before Chrissie got up.

Till now Mills had had only two interests outside boxing: his home and his Chinese restaurant. But on his recent visit to South Africa, after trekking through game reserves, he had bought himself a cine-camera. Now he proposed to make the most of his enforced inactivity by taking a delayed honeymoon trip to South Africa and combining it with photography. Chrissie wasn't initially enthusiastic, but Freddie was bubbling with excitement at the thought of the luxurious hotels and the wild animals they would see. It would have been churlish of her to refuse.

Whilst Mills became reasonably proficient with his camera, he never remotely learnt to cope with the expensive projector he installed in their home. Often when guests would be waiting to see a film of one of his fights, Freddie would be found in his den looking like an Egyptian mummy, swathed in yards of film.

Chrissie and Freddie flew to South Africa towards the end of February. It wasn't to be all honeymoon for Mills was determined to leave nothing to chance for his Woodcock challenge. Woodcock had agreed to fight Johnny Ralph in South Africa, and Mills intended to watch the contest. It would be valuable for him to see how Woodcock handled a man whom he, Mills, had already beaten.

Shortly before they left, Mills played a short part in an Arthur Askey radio revue. Having been the butt of the little comedian's jokes, the champion sang 'Mairzey Dotes' and gave a vastly over-accented impression of Charles Boyer. (At the time every amateur impressionist included Boyer, Bing Crosby and Maurice Chevalier – an ex-boxer – in his repertoire.) Mills would never become a good actor: he was unable to shed his mask of the popular man. He wasn't very talented as a music-hall artist either, but his unflagging enthusiasm and likeability so endeared him to his audiences that they overlooked his shortcomings. An ex-service friend sent him a parody of 'There's no Business like Show Business' which lampooned the greediness of boxing promoters. Mills adopted it as his theme song.

His appearance with Arthur Askey reinforced his decision to take up radio, film and television work when eventually he retired. The men and women on the lighter side of the entertainment industry tended to treat all fellow performers as long-lost friends. Freddie accepted the women's 'Hello, dahlin!' and the men's, 'Freddie! Bless your dear heart!' as sincere tributes to his popularity. He either couldn't or didn't wish to look any deeper.

Chrissie and Freddie were met in South Africa by Johnny Williams who was a close friend and whom Freddie usually employed as a sparring-partner. Surprisingly, he brought with him Don McCorkindale, Chrissie's former husband. Chrissie and Freddie had taken the young Donny McCorkindale, Chrissie and Don's son, with them on this belated honeymoon. Now the father was able for the first time for many months to see his son. No one can know today how it came about, but from then on McCorkindale stayed with the honeymooners. Surely there must have been shared memories which excluded Mills when Chrissie and McCorkindale exchanged glances? Mills wasn't particularly imaginative but when he saw them together, didn't he visualize what they must have been like at more intimate moments?

This travelling *ménage à trois* lent credence to those who, after Mills's death, suggested that there was something sexually perverse about the champion. Certainly, despite his popularity there were never any rumours of his womanizing, and the more ribald boxing hangers-on had often joked in the dressing-room about the smallness of his penis. Was it at Chrissie's wish that McCorkindale stayed with them? At the very least, the South African would have been company for her when Freddie was performing at the stag nights in the clubs. There were also the rumours at the time of the coroner's inquest that Freddie had taken his own life because he was about to be arrested for homosexual activities, which were then illegal. Bizarre as were the reasons dreamed up after his death, no one ever postulated that Freddie and McCorkindale had an homosexual affair. Indeed, the mind boggles at the mental picture of the two broken-nosed, cauliflower-eared pug-uglies in a romantic clinch.

Despite his plans, Mills did not see the Woodcock–Ralph fight because Chrissie was taken ill and had to spend three weeks in hospital. She pressed him to go but he refused to leave her, which was odd when one considers how frequently he left her on those stag nights. Perhaps, despite the public announcements of his intention to watch his next opponent, he was inwardly apprehensive as to what he might see? Certainly the ease with which Woodcock beat Ralph could have done little to enhance his confidence.

After they returned from their honeymoon, one of Mills's first visits was to Windmill Street, where he learned that the fight was already a sell-out.

Nat Seller again chose Box Hill for their training camp, and a ring was erected in the public bar as it wasn't yet warm enough to train in the open air. Daily reports on Mills's progress were issued to the press, for the fight had captured the public's imagination. Was it David and Goliath again, with the odds this time on Goliath? Or would the swashbuckling Mills be altogether too imaginative for the thick-headed Doncaster man?

One reporter tried to squeeze a story out of Chrissie's reaction to her husband fighting, forgetting perhaps that she had been brought up amongst fighters. Asked if she were going to watch the contest, Chrissie was reported as saying: 'I intend storing up all our dirty clothes so I'll have something to occupy my mind. I remember when he fought Pol Goffaux a couple of my friends came round to keep me company. But I was so nervous, I went into the lavatory and didn't come out until the fight was over.'

Pressed further, she declared – so the reporter related – 'I couldn't watch Freddie fight. I don't even enjoy watching him give exhibitions. If I'd had a daughter I might feel differently. But I've a son. I don't want to encourage him to have anything to do with the sport . . I'd hate him to think I was approving.'

Nat Seller, who understood the effects of a long lay-off, insisted that Mills should train harder for this fight than ever before. The sparring-partners were ordered to go all out. But as well as choosing them for their toughness, Seller also selected men who could help divert Freddie and leave him little time for any brooding. Again, this indicates the depth of Freddie's blue moods. Of course, most boxers are highly strung and tetchy before a major contest, and this fight was of the utmost importance to the whole of Mills's future. At the Barley Mow, it must have been rather like a prep-school outing with Johnny Williams, Joe Joachim (an Indian Olympic boxer), and Ken Shaw all forcing themselves to amuse the champion every minute he wasn't actually training.

Their efforts were augmented by the visits of many friends from the world of entertainment. Theatre personalities have always been attracted to training camps: there is something intrinsically theatrical and dramatic in the idea of a man driving himself towards exhaustion with the sole aim of pounding a rival into unconsciousness. One regular and very welcome visitor was Ann Shelton, an old and valued friend of the Broadribb family who was to play a leading role in the drama of Mills's death.

Mills trained with even more dedication than he had shown in his early fights, so that his manager and trainer both became convinced he would win. Indeed, Broadribb was so certain of the outcome that he opened negotiations for Freddie to defend the heavyweight championship against a new challenger. Nat Seller joked that if Freddie lost he would publicly eat his new horn-rimmed spectacles.

The Mills camp was so obsessed with the coming contest that they were only mildly interested to read that Lesnevich, tired of waiting for the promised return, had signed to fight Joey Maxim. Broadribb's interest was, however, awakened when he received a cable offering Mills £25,000 to meet the winner of that fight. But there was really little point in Broadribb beginning the rehearsed dance of bargaining until the Woodcock fight was out of the way. With Woodcock beaten, Mills would hold six championships and would be in an even stronger position to demand giant purses.

The BBC was extremely anxious to broadcast the Woodcock–Mills contest. With £80,000 worth of tickets already sold, radio coverage couldn't conceivably damage the takings. Nevertheless Solomons, with all the outrage of a father defending his daughter's honour, told reporters: 'For me it's a matter of principle! Principle! The BBC have offered only £250. Why should they get the fight of the century for peanuts?'

So Solomons stuck to his convenient principles and the BBC increased its modest offer. A bargain was struck and fans would be able to listen to a commentary on the fight immediately following the nine o'clock news.

The pre-fight experts forecast a Woodcock victory. Those sports writers who were able to remain cool and analytical despite the hysterical build-up were aware of Mills's capabilities, and knew his courage, but they also recalled his surrender to Lloyd Marshall. The Doncaster fighter was substantially the heavier man. They made Woodcock favourite at odds of four to one.

A surprising number of boxing columnists have extremely little knowledge of the sport and were deluded by the highly coloured stories emanating from the training-camps. They saw the contest as the cavalier against the pug-ugly; the rapier against the bludgeon. They compared Mills's confidence with Woodcock's apprehension since having his jaw broken by Joe Baksi, and eagerly accepted the odds. Frank Butler, one of the most knowledgeable of the boxing writers, based his prediction on Mills's ability to stand up to heavy punches. He said the fight would go the distance, with Mills losing on points.

Jack Solomons made the most confident prophecy of all: 'There is only one certain winner, and that's me! Forty-six thousand seats have already been sold.' As usual, he was right.

The atmosphere at the weigh-in before an important fight is always tense. This tension is often exploited by the more confident boxer or his manager. Muhammad Ali's eyeball-to-eyeball confrontation and jeers often had his opponent asking himself whether he had a vestige of a chance before he even climbed into the ring.

Since this was a heavyweight contest, neither boxer had had to 'boil down'. At the same time, the weights were important because the officials and press wanted to be sure that both boxers were well trained and had come in at their best fighting weights. Bill Turner adjusted the scales as Mills stepped on to them. There wasn't a sound. Mills looked round, noticing the serious expressions.

'Cheer up, for God's sake! It may never happen!'

There was a nervous laugh. He stepped off the scales and standing back began to sing: 'There's no business like show-business . . .' Officials thought that this was a ruse to throw the Woodcock camp off balance. It wasn't. If anything it was a reflection of Mills's own nervousness. He sang as a safety valve. He would have thought any effort to put down Woodcock beneath him.

Woodcock proved to be a stone and a half heavier, and had over an inch in reach advantage.

Mills was sharing a dressing-room with Johnny Williams who had won a preliminary contest. Mills called out to his entourage that this was just the omen he needed. People usually remember such portents only when events justify them. This was not one of those occasions, and most of those who'd been in the dressing-room failed to recall the moment.

In the first round Woodcock landed several hard blows to the body,

Sam McKeown's fairground boxing-booth where Freddie Mills learned his trade as a boxer. Mills is at the extreme left of the line-up challenging all comers

A discussion with the promoter Jack Solomons in his office

Freddie Mills, British cruiserweight champion,
in training for his first fight against
Gus Lesnevich in 1946

Mills attacking Lesnevich in the 19
world lightheavyweight title fight

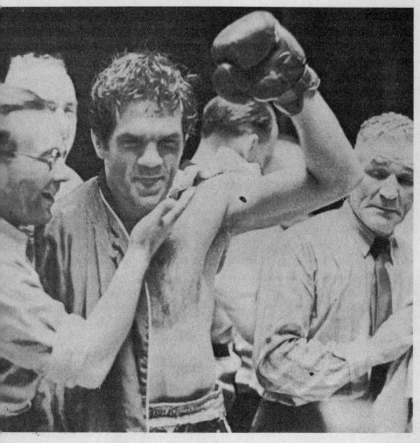

Mills, victorious over Lesnevich in 1948, is congratulated by his trainer Nat Seller on the left and his manager Ted Broadribb on the right

Mills at his training camp preparing to defend his world lightheavyweight title against Joey Maxim in 1950

Down and nearly out – the end of Freddie Mills's boxing career with his defeat by Joey Maxim in 1950

Mills owned this Chinese restaurant in partnership with Andy Ho: when it began to lose money they converted it into the Freddie Mills Nite Spot

Boxer turned promoter – Freddie Mills's first boxing promotion in London, at the Empress Hall, in 1952. Photographed with him is the boxer Don Cockell

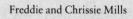
Freddie and Chrissie Mills

Joggi Villa, the Mills family home
in South London

Freddie Mills, always popular with youngsters, autographing books for delighted fans

Goslett Yard, the Soho alley behind the Freddie Mills Nite Spot where Mills's body was found in his Citroën on 25 July 1965

At home with the Krays – left to right: Ronnie, mother Vi, Reggie, and grandfather Jimmy Lee

Charlie and Eddie Richardson, leaders of the South London gang

which Mills took without showing any ill-effects and countered with a vicious left hook that shook the heavier man. Woodcock retaliated with three hard straight lefts that jerked Mills's head back. It was Woodcock's round.

Mills took the second round with his left hooks which at one stage had the Yorkshireman wobbling.

At the start of the third round, Mills again landed a heavy left hook to Woodcock's jaw. Ring-siders leant forward to see what Woodcock's reaction would be to a punch similar to that Baksi had used when knocking him out. Woodcock only shook his head and countered with a hard straight right which sent Mills back on to his heels. The more discerning fight-fans noticed that Woodcock had taken Mills's best punches and – though shaken – had remained on his feet, but Mills had been visibly distressed every time Woodcock landed. Some of those who'd backed Mills began to hedge their bets. When Mills was forced to take a count of three the crowd grew ominously silent.

By the fourth round, Woodcock's left eye was bleeding but he continued to score with hard left leads, few of which missed their target. Mills, sensing the fight was going against him, became increasingly wild. He was still a long way from being beaten and the sixth round was his best. Once again he showed his innate sportsmanship. He moved into attack, throwing a light measuring left lead. Woodcock almost rode the following left hook, but slipped, falling to the canvas, and rose awkwardly, pulling himself erect by the top rope. As he did so he was open and Mills would have been entirely justified in taking advantage of the opening. But that was not his way. Instead, he stood back until Woodcock was ready and then extended his gloves in the traditional boxing salute. Old-timers shook their heads in sorrow. The boxing-ring to them was a battle ground: you took advantage of every opportunity. There was no room for foolish chivalry.

From the sixth round onwards every punch thrown by Woodcock jarred Mills. In the eighth the lighter man was forced to take two counts. In the ninth it seemed more than likely that the referee would be forced to stop the contest to save Mills. At one moment he stood defenceless rocking on his heels as Woodcock measured him again and again, driving hard lefts and rights to the jaw.

By the start of the fourteenth round, Mills had been on the canvas four times. For most of the audience it was a relief when Woodcock threw a hard, loping left to Mills's head, dropping him for the last time. Mills took the full count resting on one knee. Then he wobbled back to his corner, a rueful half-grin on his battered face. Once again he had failed to give away weight. Once again he had taken too many punches to the head. Indeed, in this contest he had absorbed more punches than in any other three contests except his first fight with Lesnevich.

He had lost his chance of becoming heavyweight champion of his country but the manner of his losing won him even more admirers.

Describing the end of the Woodcock contest, Mills said: 'All I remember was a red mask . . . Woodcock's face. I tried to find an opening, but Bruce found it first. I remember thinking, "That's torn it," when another left and right landed either side of my head . . . I remember very little more.'

This terrible battering was received by a man who before the contest had been suffering from headaches and dizzy spells. Although he had been examined by two consultants, there is no record of his being sent for any neurological investigation before being allowed to fight again.

Once more Ted Broadribb told the press that never again would Mills be called upon to face heavyweights; now he would turn his attention to the lightheavyweight division, his own weight, where he was unbeatable. The louder Broadribb talked the more it seemed he was trying to divert attention from the defeat and focus interest on the titles Mills still held.

Press statements in the days after the fight lent support to his words: 'Brave Mills'; 'Mills fights to last breath'; Defeated but with glory'.

Mills had earned his reputation for fearlessness despite his surrender to Lloyd Marshall. But one must ask whether, having been sent into the ring once too often, he had used up his courage? By the night he was found shot dead in Goslett Yard, had he expended his stock of that virtue?

In a contest which raised little interest in the Mills camp, Joey Maxim defeated Gus Lesnevich. The Americans now pressed even more vigorously for Mills to defend his title against Maxim. But Mills had been paid more than £14,000 for fighting Woodcock, and if he fought again too soon he would only receive a few shillings in the pound after paying taxation.

Broadribb summed up the situation succinctly: 'Mills isn't getting any younger. We'd rather he defended his championship this year than next. But, as things stand at the present, we'd be fighting for almost nothing even if he were paid £20,000.'

The manager, trying to find a way out of the impasse, suggested to the Americans they should pay Mills in instalments spread over the next five years. The Americans were prepared to accept this condition but the British tax inspector wasn't so agreeable.

Broadribb now sought another solution. He would sell Mills's contract to an American manager who would then act as the promoter. Mills would stay in the USA for some months and so – he hoped – would avoid British taxation. Unfortunately the American promoters were not as enthusiastic over the plan as was Broadribb, who was offered only £1,250 for Mills's contract. Apparently in the States, as in England, it was realized that Mills was coming to the end of his fighting, and earning, career.

Broadribb peddled his idea elsewhere, but the taxation stumbling-block seemed insurmountable. If the Americans didn't ransack Mills's purse, the British would.

American promoters don't easily accept defeat, and the promoter who had originally been prepared to buy Mills's contract went ahead with his plans as though his offer had been accepted. He announced that any day now Mills would be landing in the States to fight under his banner. He cabled Mills that he had three contests already arranged for him: the first against Tommy Yarosz, the second against Joey Maxim and the third with the winner of the Ezzard Charles--Gus Lesnevich match.

Broadribb immediately flew out to the States to try and safeguard Mills's interests and reputation. By the time he returned to the UK he found another offer awaiting him: Solomons proposed that Mills should meet Joey Maxim for the title in London . . . but not till next year. The delay would eliminate the taxation problems and would ensure that Mills fought in front of his own crowd. The only snag was that by the time they climbed into the ring Mills would be a full year older and wouldn't have fought for well over six months. Mills was a boxer who needed to fight regularly to be at his best.

By the end of August all the negotiations had been completed and Maxim's manager announced to the press: 'The fight is definitely on. The signing of contracts is a mere formality.'

Meanwhile the contract between Mills and Broadribb had expired. Mills initially said he didn't need to sign a contract as he intended to continue fighting for his father-in-law, but Broadribb considered this suggestion 'unbusinesslike', and a new contract covering the next three years was eventually drawn up. Both men realized that this would see the end of Mills's boxing career.

The six months' delay did not please the Americans, who had sound reason for their anger. Several outstanding contenders for Mills's crown would now have to wait in the wings lest they were beaten and so lost their chance of the big pay-day. The NBA – the main American control body – thereupon passed a resolution to the effect that if Mills did not defend his world title within ninety days, the championship would be declared vacant and they would stage their own eliminating contests leading to the crowning of a new champion.

Jack Solomons, a most wily operator, set a date for the contest, after discussions with the taxation authorities, which both carried Mills into the next taxation year and was just within the limits set by the American control board.

The hangers-on of the boxing world are usually know-alls with remarkably little real insight into the sport. Although Mills owed his fitness for numerous contests to Nat Seller, his trainer, well-wishers from the world of boxing and of show-business now assured him that he was wasting money and didn't need anyone to tell him how to get fit. They reminded him that he had been fighting for more than a decade and during the war had been a fully qualified PT instructor. 'Surely you can train yourself? Don't you know better than anyone else what you need?'

The words of the flatterers echoed in Mills's mind, and the more he thought about it, the more logical the argument seemed. Finally he told the press: 'I know better than anyone else how I feel during training. Some days I don't feel like boxing and a walk away from the gym would be better for me. In the past with a full-time trainer I have been forced to box publicly. Now I'll train myself and be fitter because of it.'

Boxers need confidants to whom they can talk without reserve. When asked about this aspect of his decision, Mills said: 'I've Frank Duffet as my adviser and masseur. He's very intelligent and will look after my interests as if they were his own.' Duffet remained a close friend and business associate for the rest of Mills's life.

Nat Seller accepted Mills's decision. There was nothing he could do about it, since he was contracted from fight to fight. But it was a shabby reward for a long and loyal association. Fortunately shortly before he got down to full training, Mills's basic loyalty reasserted itself. He called a press conference to say he had changed his mind and that once again Seller would be in charge of the camp.

By the time Mills and Seller were settled in the Barley Mow only four weeks remained before what was to be Mills's last fight. Before leaving for his training camp, Mills spent a quiet Christmas at Joggi Villa with Chrissie. With all the press writers talking about Mills's future contests, Chrissie was the only person close to him thinking about his retirement. Although she had spent her whole life surrounded by boxers and their families, she hated the sport and what it did to brave men. Boxers whom she had hero-worshipped were now stumbling punch-drunks. Her husband was strong, healthy and, despite his broken nose and cauliflower ear, still good-looking: she wanted him to stay that way. But Freddie refused to listen to her. As he saw it, men earned the money and women looked after the home and children. Chrissie has said since that if he had listened to her he would have given up even before he fought Maxim.

During the Christmas holiday, Mills was irritated to read that in the lightheavyweight rankings published in the *Ring* he was listed only third, below Joey Maxim and Archie Moore. He considered this a studied American insult and became even more determined to retain his title.

Over recent months he had been in light training, but training is not the same as fighting. It was more than six months since he had faced Woodcock and taken far too many hard blows to the head. The older a boxer becomes the more difficult he finds it to drive himself to complete fitness. Instead of looking forward to sparring, Mills now had to make an effort not to let his mind wander when in the ring. What had previously been a pleasure had become hard labour. Now thirty-one, he realized he was ring-rusty, and doubts spawned shadows in his mind. Could he once again bring himself to that vital tautness of mind and body?

Freddie Mills refused to face the fact that he had had enough of boxing. He told himself: 'A few more fights and I shall be able to retire with enough money to live well for the rest of my life. If I hung up my gloves now, how long would they remember me?' He told friends: 'I've every intention of remaining world champion. I'll still be fighting when 1950 is over.'

Whilst Maxim was crossing the Atlantic, the Cincinnati promoter who'd tried to take over Mills's contract issued a statement declaring that he owned exclusive rights to the British boxer's services and intended to take legal action to prevent the London contest taking place. Solomons brushed this threat aside: he had already sold 16,000 seats, and the fight would definitely take place. If boxers fought as viciously as promoters, the fight-fans would never have grounds for complaint.

The British sports writers turned Maxim into an old-time villain. Whilst Mills would be fighting for the glory of his country, Maxim was a mean man fighting solely for dollars. Maxim had employed a personal friend as trainer so as to save having to pay wages. Although he was a multi-millionaire, Maxim still ran a second-hand car sales organization. Jack Benny was generous in comparison.

In truth, Joey Maxim was a most likeable, intelligent man who became extremely popular with everyone who got to know him.

The pre-match hype went on. Don Cockell, one of Maxim's sparring-partners, swore that the American was the fastest boxer he had ever faced. From Box Hill reports were leaked that Seller had repeatedly had to shout to Mills to ease up, as sparring-partners walked out rather than accept Mills's vicious left hooks. Ted Broadribb told the press that Mills had never been so fit and couldn't lose.

Perhaps the British trainer and manager protested too much, because the bookmakers – not men to be swayed by sentiment – offered odds of nine to four against Mills. By the time the preliminary fighters were in the ring, the odds had shortened to two to one on the American. Many of the sports writers who had watched Maxim in training took up these odds. They wrote that the American was wide open to a left hook, and though Mills may have been out of action too long for his own good, his left hook was a reflex action. And when it landed . . .

Writer Lainson Wood was less impressed. He reminded his readers that Mills had taken too many hard punches in recent contests and questioned whether his legs would last fifteen rounds. Geoffrey Simpson of the *Daily Mail* also predicted a Maxim victory.

The time comes when the bell rings for the first round and pre-fight prophecies matter no longer. On 24 January 1950 Freddie Mills faced Joey Maxim. He lost the contest and five of his teeth. He was knocked out in the tenth round.

To the ring-siders it appeared that Mills might win a sensational victory when he landed a terrific left hook in the very first minute of the fight. Maxim grabbed Mills and clung on desperately until the referee prised them apart. Mills followed this with another left to the body and a right to the jaw. In training Maxim had looked a little frail, but even after this punishment he seemed surprisingly confident. He shook his head and moved forward.

In the third round Maxim took the initiative and reached Mills's jaw again and again with hard lefts. Then he landed with a jolting right upper-cut. Though Mills fought back, he had been hurt. In the sixth Mills's head was exploded backwards by a similar blow. He said later: 'I felt my teeth moving about. I was in a daze.' In his corner before the seventh round, Nat Seller pulled out two teeth.

Mills, still dazed when the bell brought him out of his corner, was too slow to avoid another upper-cut. In the next interval Seller extracted another tooth which had become impacted in his gum shield.

Mills had little memory of the rest of the fight. He fought on by instinct. He couldn't recall the punch which knocked him out and only regained consciousness as he was being sick in the dressing-room.

Usually a defeated fighter's dressing-room is empty but for a morose trainer cutting off the sweat-stained bandages and plasters from the boxer's hands. The claque which invades the potential winner's dressing-room before a contest quickly transfers its allegiance to the other man. This fight proved an exception. Again and again the dressing-room door opened to admit personalities of the theatre, TV and films as well as genuine admirers – all come to congratulate Mills on his courage.

Asked later why he had lost, Mills was silent for a few seconds. Then he raised his head. 'I've never really been the same since that first Lesnevich fight. When a boxer takes a caning like that his days are numbered . . . even though he mayn't realize it at the time.'

# 9

Most of Mills's admirers wanted him to retire but hesitated to put their hopes into words. It would be difficult enough for him to accept that he was no longer the champion of the world without any added suggestion that he had no future in the ring at all. Mills must have wondered whether after his overwhelming defeat he would still have a following, being too intelligent not to know that fame is fleeting.

When the doctor of the Board of Control had cleaned out his mouth and given him pain-killers, Mills pushed his way through the throng outside the dressing-room door, excusing himself for leaving, and drove home to Chrissie. A tea-pot and cup were laid out ready for him on the kitchen table. For once Freddie said 'no' to the tea. His mouth was too sore.

Frank Duffet was the only intimate other than Chrissie still with him by the next morning. He lounged in an easy chair without speaking. Mills sensed his masseur's lack of composure.

'Well?'

Duffet didn't speak.

'Didn't do well, did I?'

Looking back over the years Duffet has said that he believed Mills already knew the answer. But, at the time, he thought Mills would cling, like a child to his favourite toy, to the boxing honours he still held. Though he had lost the world title, he still held the British Empire and European championships. As long as he held them he would be admired and lionized, and even though the experts might consider him finished, his fans, the public, would still pay to see him face new challengers. Such thoughts would be urging Mills to fight again.

However inadequate his performance against Maxim, he could have had at least three more lucrative contests. Frank Duffet knew this: Mills knew it. Would he take advantage of these financial opportunities while knowing that more boxing might wreck his health? From now on there would be no easy money. Crowds would be going to see him beaten and humiliated, not to knock out push-overs.

Frank Duffet summed up the situation: 'Freddie had passed his best. There is only one way after that . . . downhill. There's nothing more tragic than a boxer who's been good finishing up as just another punk. A man of Mills's class must go out while people remember him at his best. I said to him that day: "Freddie, you'd be wise to get out now. There's no point in going in there and getting beaten by bums who shouldn't be in the same ring with you. Go out while you're still someone."'

Frank Duffet had chosen his words carefully. It was the fear of becoming a 'no-one' and forfeiting his popularity that Mills dreaded more than inactivity or losing his earning power. Years later, Duffet could still recall Mills sitting there listening, his face swollen and both eyes bruised purple.

'He didn't give me any argument. He weighed it up in his own mind. I know that afterwards he talked it over with Chrissie, and he may have consulted Ted Broadribb. But the decision was his alone. Inside him, he knew he'd come to the end.'

As soon as Broadribb had left the dressing-room the night before, he'd been surrounded by reporters.

'Will Mills hang up his gloves now?'

'Will you, as manager, allow him to take any more hidings?'

'Are you going to ask for a return?'

'When will he defend his British championship?'

'Is he finished?'

The manager had held up his hand for silence, and when he could be heard clearly, he'd said: 'As Mills's father-in-law, I would say to him: "Finish with the game."' He paused then added as a safety clause: 'But it's *his* livelihood, after all. It's the only thing he knows . . .'

Broadribb failed to mention that it was also his own livelihood and that Mills had made more money for him than any other two fighters he had handled. A manager is a boxer's personal representative. Though he may have bought a boxer's contract from another manager, he doesn't *own* the fighter. If Mills had decided to fight again, Broadribb would have had either to continue to represent his interests or to have cancelled their contract. He could have done nothing to prevent Mills boxing. Had he tried to do so he could have been accused of depriving his fighter of the right to earn his living, and Mills could have appealed to the Board of

Control for his contract with his manager to be rescinded.

The next morning, Mills's decision to retire made headlines. His own summing-up was widely quoted: 'I'm washed up . . . that's all there is to it.'

Broadribb called another press conference, this time an official one. He wanted to turn the decision to advantage. He told the reporters: 'We had a long family talk and agreed that it's time for Freddie to pack it in. If Freddie is prevailed upon to change his mind, I'm afraid he'll have to manage himself. I'll continue to look after his business affairs if he wants me to. But no more boxing. That's final.'

It sounded well. It read well. However, Mills's manager was first and foremost a businessman, and his business was boxing. He'd been extremely impressed by Joey Maxim's performance against his boy, and had described the American as 'boxing like a master'. Even before the public had time to read his lofty sentiments, he'd made an offer for a part-share in the new champion's contract.

The other man who had a financial interest in Mills, Jack Solomons, said that for his part he welcomed the boxer's decision. Solomons had the reputation of being a man who read percentage signs better than he did his wife's letters. There is little doubt that he could have persuaded Mills to defend his British and European championships. Mills, always grateful and loyal to Solomons for giving him the chance to earn big money, would have found it difficult to resist the temptation of 'just one more'. Yet, when told of Mills's decision, Solomons merely remarked: 'I think he is very wise indeed.'

From that day onwards, Solomons was always available when Mills wanted advice or guidance on promoting his own tournaments. When Mills's elder daughter, Susan, was christened, Solomons became her godfather. Solomons' critics – and they were legion – would have been amused at the connotations today of the word 'godfather'.

When Mills retired, Solomons had no British-born fighter capable of drawing the crowds. As he had done a few months earlier, the promoter appealed to the BBBC to amend their rules so that on his next bill he could match two foreign boxers: Maxim and a suitable opponent from the Continent or America. Because of his victory over Mills, Maxim, the new champion, would find enthusiastic support among British fight-fans.

The day the press announced his retirement, Mills was having his mouth treated. His dentist discovered that the damage was far more serious than had been thought. A bone in the jaw had been shattered and he needed an immediate operation to remove the splinters, after which he would have to have three false teeth fitted. Mills took no pleasure from press reports that Maxim had also suffered damage to his mouth and had been taken to hospital. He liked and respected his conqueror. He telephoned Jack Solomons to find out the name of the hospital, only to learn that the whole story was the product of the fertile mind of a Fleet Street hack.

Mills had been paid £10,000 as his share of the purse. Today that would be a trivial sum for a world championship, and the winner would also receive subsidiary revenue in sponsorship, TV fees and payments for personal appearances. But in those days there were few spin-offs, and the purse was considered generous. Indeed, one critic wrote that the world must be mad to pay such a terrific sum to watch two men try to knock each other senseless. This philosopher, estimating that Mills had earned £345 per minute, pointed out that this was more than William Shakespeare had earned from all his plays.

Others tried to assess how much money Mills had made during his fighting career and, more important, how much he'd managed to retain out of his purses. One sportswriter suggested that Mills had well over £30,000 in his bank, apart from the mansion on Denmark Hill and his half-share in a Chinese restaurant.

Defeat is always bitter, but within days Mills's natural ebullience had re-asserted itself. Within a week he was ready to appear with his opponent on the stage of the Saville Theatre on behalf of the British Professional Boxers' Association. Mills, though lisping badly, sang his usual theme song. Then as the audience's applause died down, he remarked: 'It's good to know you recognize me standing up.'

When Joey Maxim left for the States, Mills saw him off from Paddington. As he walked back from the platform surrounded by pressmen, he came face to face with Winston Churchill who was on his way to speak in Cardiff. Churchill took his cigar out of his mouth with one hand while patting Mills on the shoulder with the other. 'Very plucky . . . very plucky indeed.'

Mills gulped. He was seldom embarrassed and usually tried to cover any sign of such an emotion with a joke. Now, almost without knowing what he was saying, he replied: 'So are you, sir.'

Churchill laughed loudly.

Mills, for the moment afraid he might have given offence, stammered quickly: 'I'm sorry I've a red tie on . . . if I'd known I was going to meet you I'd have worn my blue.'

Although Mills was now an ex-world champion, the invitations to make personal appearances were just as frequent. He opened fêtes, he visited hospitals, gave prizes at schools, boxed at youth clubs and sang in night-clubs. He didn't have a good voice but the crowds applauded just the same.

But while he was kept busy and was earning quite a reasonable income, he was making no use of his many years' experience garnered in the ring. He now contemplated taking out a manager's licence and talked enthusiastically to Frank Duffet about making a barn-storming tour of the British Isles searching for a cruiserweight who, under his management, would win back the championship he had lost.

Mills's fears of being forgotten were ill-founded for almost every day a national newspaper reported the latest Mills adventure or carried the story of a radio or TV appearance. Radio and television producers realized Mills was still so popular that if they gave him time to tell boxing anecdotes or talk about his ring experiences they were assured of substantial listening and viewing figures. In the entertainment world, he earned himself a reputation for brash impudence. Once he embarrassed a television interviewer by not only mentioning the name of his Chinese restaurant but actually giving its address.

A television producer engaged Mills as a boxing commentator. He had a pleasant voice, was good-looking and popular, but he was too much a self-publicist to be a good commentator. He sold himself rather than trying to bring alive the fight he was watching. After two try-outs his contract wasn't extended.

He applied to the Board for, and was granted, a manager's licence. The Board could hardly refuse him for, apart from his boxing record, he was well-respected for his honesty and straightforwardness. However in order to apply for a licence, the would-be manager had to provide the Board with the name of a professional boxer who would fight under his management. This could create a somewhat Gilbertian situation. At that time the area boards to whom applications had to be made consisted of managers, trainers, boxers and promoters. If a licence was refused, the boxers cited as prepared to sign up with the applicant were left managerless. So it wasn't unknown, if the would-be manager was called in and told that he must get more experience before applying again, for the room to empty as all the other managers present headed for the phones to sign up the boxers concerned. To qualify for the licence Mills had accepted, almost as a gift from his father-in-law and former manager, a promising twenty-year-old Irish-Liverpool heavyweight, Irish O'Connor.

But Mills joined a large number of former boxers who have failed as managers. Ted Broadribb was one of the few really top-class boxers who succeeded. The champion boxer operates through instinct rather than thought: he reacts rather than plans. I once asked the late Jimmy Wilde, the Ghost with a Hammer in his Hand, how he managed to punch so devastatingly when he was so puny. 'I don't know,' he answered. 'I just did. When I saw an opening, I just put my fist through it.'

It is the boxer who *almost* reaches the top who makes the best manager or teacher. Usually he had to think about what he was doing rather than depend solely on his reflex reactions. His approach had to be cerebral, not instinctive. Champions-turned-managers invariably try to mould their fighters into copies of themselves: it's all they know. Then they are disappointed when their charges are beaten. As a manager, Ted Kid Lewis used to send his boys out of their corners with orders to punch, keep punching . . . and punch some more. He was angry with them when they failed to match his genius for aggression.

Mills made no profit out of managing. After some months, on Duffet's advice, he handed in his licence and applied instead for one as promoter. With Duffet advising him, he chose Bristol as his centre, remembering that there they looked upon him as a West Countryman.

After Mills's death, Duffet described how in their early days of promotion they had no organization and had to do everything themselves. 'We started at the football ground. Mills used to go down a fortnight before the show and try to tie up all the loose ends. On the afternoon of the fights we'd get all the local kids to help put up the seats. Freddie would always horse around with them, running races, pretending to spar with them and tossing them up in the air. They all loved him. He always nursed his popularity.'

Mills was unlucky on the night of his first promotion in May 1951. Open-air boxing in Britain has always been at the mercy of the elements, and that night heavy rain restricted the gate to 6,000 which was not nearly 'break-even money'.

Mills persevered, but by the end of the year he realized he had to look elsewhere. Fortunately he was still making money from personal appearances. When asked why he still gave his services free to so many charities, he answered: 'I like it. I don't go just because they ask me. I'm interested in helping. I spend hours working for boys' clubs and I enjoy every minute of it. I feel I'm putting something back into the game.'

His radio work also began to be recognized and he was making regular appearances on the Dickie Henderson and the Ben Lyons programmes. A film producer meeting Freddie at a party noticed his wide popularity and thought that his appearance in one of his productions would provide good publicity. He cast Mills as a boxer on the skids, a punch-drunk. The promoter, having watched the rushes, described Freddie as 'a natural'. The ex-champion's warmth and enthusiasm covered the meagreness of his talent, and from then on he was always eager to accept film parts however small.

The theme of the film was the need at the time for a better blood-transfusion service. Having completed his part, Mills worked actively, not only to promote the film but to encourage the public to offer their blood.

His Chinese restaurant was also doing reasonably well under Andy Ho, even though the gloss had faded a little and fewer celebrities dropped in to see Mills.

Eventually Mills and Frank Duffet found a suitable hall in which to promote matches during the winter. A new ice-skating arena had opened in Southampton, and Mills hired it. His promotions there began to make money. Solomons, watching his efforts with interest, suggested that Freddie should turn his attention to London. Since he hadn't the drawing-cards to mount 'Solomons-sized' shows, Solomons thought Mills should take over the Empress Hall in Earl's Court.

His first promotion in London featured Yolande Pompey, the West Indian fighter, against the Danish champion. To help the publicity Mills invited Dr Edith Summerskill MP, the arch-critic of boxing, to be his guest. For years Dr Summerskill had been preaching on the dangers of boxers becoming punch-drunk. She declined being made into a publicity stunt. 'I regard Mr Mills's invitation in the same light as one I received from Mr Solomons some time ago.' She added: 'I'm sorry that simple women go to see their sons fighting. But I know the majority of women take the same view as I do: boxing should be banned before more youths suffer brain damage.'

Although I was an inspector of the BBBC, I agreed with her. I met her in the House of Commons to discuss what could be done to make boxing safer and in the course of our conversation, she told me: 'I'm glad normal women never go to fights.'

I said this wasn't true.

'It's only women who want to be seen with men with money who attend tournaments.'

I suggested that, far from that being right, more and more women were watching boxing and that perhaps they were sexually excited by the sight of two half-clad men hitting each other. She refused to admit that such an idea was possible.

Our discussions proved unproductive.

In 1956 Mills and Chrissie had their second daughter, Amanda.

In the years immediately following his retirement from the ring, Mills gave up more and more of his time to helping others. He still needed – or felt he needed – popularity. Chrissie appealed to him repeatedly to spend more time at home with their daughters, but though he enjoyed home life he desperately missed having fans all around him. He had to have constant reassurance that everybody still knew who he was and admired him. Searching out new causes to sponsor, he found one in the poor conditions experienced by prisoners in Dartmoor. At the 'Moor' he boxed an exhibition with the padre and afterwards appealed to his audience from the ring to donate blood. Mills's enthusiasm often carried him away. If he had delved a little deeper he would have found that few of the inmates would have been accepted as donors because of malnutrition.

Mills had always had many admirers among authors, scriptwriters and newspapermen. Remembering his amusing one-liners, the *Graphic* asked him to write a regular column on boxing. When Honore Pratesi of Marseilles died after a contest against the Zulu altar-boy, Jake Tuli, the former world champion wrote that a man who had had scores of fights was no more likely to be killed in the ring than men who had only climbed through the ropes three or four times. 'I am a former world champion. I had almost a hundred fights – all of them hard ones. My answer is that boxing is as safe as it can be. Otherwise, how would it survive in this humanitarian age?'

How indeed?

Explaining further, he wrote: 'No fighter goes into the ring without a doctor's examination. A doctor is always at the ring-side. In Britain a fighter has only to lose four contests and his ring activities are checked forthwith . . .'

Boxing is safer today than it ever was; there is no disputing that. But every man who boxes risks a blow which can kill him almost instantly or an accumulation of punches which can damage his brain. Dr Peter Harvey, the neurologist, has said: 'No doctor can say that in this round one of the contestants will not suffer irreversible brain damage or, indeed, death.'

Mills defended the sport so vigorously that it wasn't surprising that the Board helped him in every way possible to succeed as a promoter.

At thirty-four years of age, Mills was tempted to make a come-back.

Tonypandy Tommy Farr, who'd done so much to restore the reputation of British heavyweights after 'horizontal heavyweight' Phil Scott had made them a laughing-stock, had returned to the ring. After twelve contests of which he lost only three, he challenged Don Cockell for the British title, and the publicity surrounding this started Mills thinking. He told doubters: 'If Tommy can beat Cockell and then prove too good for my friend Johnny Williams, I shall seriously think about coming back. I could make more money in three fights than I can promoting seven shows. I hope to live till I'm eighty . . . I don't intend to sit back and do nothing.'

Chrissie and Frank Duffet tried to talk him out of the idea, but Mills could be extremely stubborn. He argued that he was five years younger than Farr, who had been out of the ring for several years, and had kept in strict training. If the fans would pay to see the rotund Farr fight, then surely they would flock to watch their great favourite make a return? He argued more to convince himself than to persuade Chrissie and Duffet. He didn't stress that he needed to fight financially because his Chinese restaurant and his promotions were both losing money.

Peter Wilson of the *Daily Mirror* reminded Mills of a passage in the champion's own autobiography, *Twenty Years*. Referring to his first fight with Lesnevich, he had written: 'Even now when at home I put on that particular film, it gives me quite a turn and, from my experience, I should say that no fighter can take such punishment on the chin and hope to be the same afterwards. Punching like that really shakes up the brain and cannot possibly do it any good.'

No doubt at the time Mills was convinced he was telling the truth, but time has a way of eradicating unpleasant memories or blurring their edges so that the good moments stand out and the bad ones fade. An ex-soldier, recalling thirty years later those heady days of war with their comradeship and excitement, will conveniently forget the terror, degradation, dirt and discomfort which were part of his daily life. So it was with Freddie Mills. After only four years out of the ring, he forgot the blows he had taken and their after-effects. He forgot his feelings when vomiting into the hand-basin in his dressing-room after being knocked out by Lloyd Marshall. He even forgot the boos as he'd crawled through the ropes towards the safety of the dressing-room. He remembered only the introductory fanfares as he stood in the spotlight, and heard again the cheering and the applause as the audience rose to him. He could recall word for word the MC's introductions. He relived the thrill of the moment when the bell went for the first round and he left his stool for the centre of the ring.

His dream of a successful return to the ring was lent substance when he read in the sporting press that Archie Moore had taken the title from Joey Maxim. This seemed an ideal moment for him to challenge for the championship once again. But his views and arguments didn't receive as wide publicity as he'd anticipated. Cynics had heard all these arguments before from other washed-up pugilists, out of whose return fights had grown the boxing legend: 'They never come back.'

Frank Duffet risked destroying their friendship by arguing strongly against the comeback. He told Mills that he was chancing his hard-won reputation against ridicule. 'Surely you want the public to remember you as you were and not as an ageing fighter with slow reflexes and telegraphed punches?'

Mills wouldn't listen to Duffet or Chrissie. He was like that greyhound 'in the slips, straining upon the start'. He could scent the wintergreen of the dressing-room; he could hear the cheers of the crowd; he could feel the power in his fists as they were bandaged, transforming them from hands into lethal weapons.

While he was dreaming of his comeback, Mills was trying to organize a tour of Korea to entertain British troops, hoping to have Randy Turpin and Johnny Williams with him. Chrissie persevered in her arguments against his making a return, but the best he would promise her was that he wouldn't make a final decision until he got back to England. 'I'll box an exhibition with Randy and see how I go. If I'm fit, then . . .'

The projected tour never materialized. The American soldiers and their British allies found themselves too busy defending themselves against the Koreans to watch boxing.

Fortunately, perhaps, Mills was at the ring-side when Tommy Farr faced Don Cockell. It wasn't the defeat of the pride of Wales which shocked Mills, but the nature of the débâcle. When Mills returned from Nottingham he wrote in his column: 'It was all rather tragic. It showed that youth gets the better of age in boxing. So I'll rest on my laurels and stick to promoting.'

His friends breathed a sigh of relief.

However within three months of his decision he took part in a different kind of contest in which words were substituted for gloves. *The Times* of 16 June 1953 carried a report of a libel action brought by Mr Frederick Mills, Mr Jack Solomons and Mr Edward Broadribb in respect of an article appearing in the *Manchester Evening News*. Two years earlier, writing of a future contest in which one of the opponents was to outweigh the other substantially, a journalist had referred to the Freddie Mills v.

Joe Baksi contest using the expression 'carve up'.

The three plaintiffs assumed the expression to have the same meaning as is accepted in boxing jargon, and the barrister representing them claimed in court that to say: 'It was a carve up,' would have been exactly the same as saying: 'The fight was fixed.'

The *Manchester Evening News* had tried to prevent the case reaching court by publishing an apology, but it wasn't accepted. Naturally the lawyers enjoyed the play with words and after much laughter in court a settlement was agreed.

Mills welcomed the damages, for promoting had become an even more hazardous activity than formerly. The Government had introduced a thirty-three per cent tax on public shows, and in the UK the number of boxing promotions that year dropped to less than seventy from an annual two hundred.

Although he still continued to promote at the Empress Hall, Mills realized that he would have to find some other way to augment his income from personal appearances and the restaurant. He considered everything. He wasn't over-proud and, agreeing at one point to take part in an ice-show, he was photographed for the bills sliding across the ice on his bottom. Freddie Mills the ex-boxer was prepared to play Freddie Mills the clown so long as he was paid, and the fans laughed and liked him.

He was invited to speak against Dr Edith Summerskill MP in a debate promoted by a society of barristers. Jack Solomons was the principal speaker defending boxing, and Freddie for once was to be the second.

Opening the debate, Dr Summerskill spoke of the fragility of the brain and concentrated on the ethical aspects of the industry. Jack Solomons recounted how he had raised thousands of pounds for charity by running boxing shows, and whilst admitting there were *some* grounds for criticism, he stated that thousands of people enjoyed the sport: 'Surely they're not all crazy!'

Mills, taking over the defence, was asked by Dr Summerskill about his cauliflower ear. He said he had acquired it playing rugby. Fortunately none of the listening barristers had been properly briefed, for no one challenged this statement. (The expression 'economical with the truth' hadn't yet been made popular by the 'Spycatcher' case.) At one stage in his prepared speech he lost his thread, and Dr Summerskill seized her opportunity. 'Has your memory gone?' she asked sympathetically.

Mills replied quickly that in his whole boxing career he had met only one punch-drunk boxer and this poor creature hadn't been British.

Although he had promised Duffet that he would accept fewer unpaid invitations, Freddie found it difficult to say 'no'. Asked to take part in a brains trust, he agreed without finding out details, but subsequently learned that it was to raise funds for the Conservative Party. He withdrew immediately. 'In the first place I know nothing about politics. In the second, as a promoter and showman I can't afford to get mixed up in things like that.'

On television he played the clown again as stooge to red-nosed Charlie Cairoli, allowing the musician to pour buckets of water into his trousers.

Mills was resilient, and apparently never allowed financial worries to prey on his mind. He was, after all, still in popular demand. He was writing articles. His name was in the press. He was making personal appearances. He was performing in cabarets – he appeared in denim trousers and sweat-shirt at the Dorchester as the bruiser who answered foolishly when asked awkward questions by the egghead . . . me!

In 1956 he received his most exciting invitation when he was asked to box an exhibition bout at Buckingham Palace. The canvas was the lush grass of the rose garden, and he sparred with Johnny Williams. A coloured photograph of the occasion became one of Jack Solomons' most prized possessions, and was used after Mills's death as the frontispiece for the programme, 'The Freddie Mills Night in Aid of the Dependants of the late Freddie Mills' on 1 February 1966.

# 10

FREDDIE Mills's Chinese Restaurant, after a successful few years, had started to lose money. Having a celebrated owner was no longer enough to bring in the customers, and the competition from new Chinese restaurants throughout the West End had intensified. So Freddie Mills, with some doubts, decided instead to go into the night-club business, which was booming. An industrial psychologist, having assessed Mills's nature and talents, and appraised his background and experiences over the last twenty years, would almost certainly have recommended this step. His experience of the catering trade plus his convivial, spontaneous temperament made him an ideal host.

Yet when Mills and Andy Ho decided to make the change, they may have unknowingly been condemning the ex-boxer to death.

In the post-war years vice, illicit drinking, illegal gambling and peddling drugs were earning fortunes for those ready to exploit the demand. For years Londoners had lived in darkness. It was not the law which had limited relaxation and licence as much as wartime restrictions and the black-out. Now men, with eyes glistening at the prospect of easy profits, had only to find suitable premises and spend a little money on decoration and publicity to make profits. There was no shortage of potential customers. Men and women who had for the war years lived on the knife-edge of emotion were returning to the security – and the greyness – of civil life.

The ex-pilot who had hunted bandits in the clouds quitted his cockpit for a daily ride on the tube and became an insurance agent. After the first exuberant relief at his survival, boredom and dissatisfaction overwhelmed him. The servicemen had all talked about what they were going to do after the war, but reality soon dispelled dreams. In the words of T.S. Eliot: 'Humankind cannot bear very much reality'.

In the precious hours outside his nine to five-thirty job, the ex-serviceman searched for his lost comradeship. He desperately needed an audience which would help him relive his heady past. In the afternoon drinking-clubs he could find his counterparts, ex-officers and ex-NCOs who treated each other to 'pinko-gino's', talked louder than was necessary and bragged of the importance of the work they were currently doing. None of them believed – or needed to believe – the other's lies. In the night-clubs, when they could afford the entrance fees, they found women who would not only listen to their wartime escapades, but who would giggle at their jokes. If the money was available, these 'hostesses' would allow their escorts to take them home when the club closed at three or four in the morning. Although the sex was strictly commercial, the euphemism 'hostess' helped preserve the vital illusion of seduction.

Prostitution thrived during the war; the black-out had proved profitable for at least one profession. Gambling joints also proliferated. Vice was big business, and small gangs specialized in specific areas of crime. Dog didn't eat dog . . . at first. There was enough for all without any gang warfare. They only fought when one gang encroached on another's pitch.

The Maltese brothers, the Messinas, soon controlled most of the prostitutes and the name Messina became prominent among the aristocracy of London crime. The Sabina brothers specialized in 'protecting' bookmakers and exploiting the racing fraternity. If a bookmaker dared decline their offer of protection, his pitch on the course would be over-run and his representatives assaulted. In the long run it was easier, cheaper and safer to pay up.

At first the gangsters did keep to their own areas of speciality. But inevitably they became greedy and jealous of each other. The gangs organizing prostitution noted the rich profits made by the protection-racketeers. The protection boys envied the brothel-keepers. The brothel-keepers eyed the money being raked in by the gambling syndicates. And all of them preyed on the night-club owners who worked almost within the law, providing customers with what they wanted, legally. To attract customers a night-club had to have a luxurious décor. This was expensive, and made the club extremely susceptible to wrecking. The clubs relied on wealthy, well-known patrons to introduce new members, and the ideal client was also the person most likely to hurry away at the first hint of strong-arm methods or scandal.

For many club owners the only safe path, other than paying the exorbitant demands of the crooks, was to 'tip' legal protectors . . . the police. West End Central police force became extremely susceptible to sweeteners. It would be wrong, however to suggest that only in Central London were the police ready to be 'reasonable'. At the same time, the Richardson brothers, Charlie and Eddie, were alleged to be paying more than £1,000 a week in Greenwich to be left in peace.

With the boom in business, the gangs all became efficient and looked upon themselves as commercial enterprises. The leaders were the managing directors, con-men became entrepreneurs.

Two of the gang leaders became more powerful than all the others; indeed, more powerful than had ever before been known in Britain. One of them was Billy Hill, a quiet, businesslike organizer who would rather make a deal than get himself embroiled in violence. The other was Jack 'Spot' Comer, a gangster who always sported a Churchill-sized cigar and believed that violence was a weapon which could be wielded profitably. Hill, although an ex-thief with a long prison record, was a smooth, almost polished man. Jack Spot was the East End villain, vindictive and vicious.

Spot and Hill used each other for what each had to offer. Their respect and dislike were mutual. When the inevitable break came, Billy Hill was ready: he could do without Spot but Spot could not do without him. To survive with any 'face', Spot desperately needed allies. He found them in the Kray brothers who had been terrorizing clubs, pubs, cafés and small businesses in the East End. It was through Jack Spot's withdrawal from the fray and Billy Hill's ultimate retirement – not attributable to Spot or his allies – that the way was opened up for the Krays to move 'up West' in the 1960s.

In view of the subsequent rumours throughout the underworld linking the Krays to the death of Freddie Mills, it is necessary to trace the careers and characters of these brothers, both almost illiterate, who are now serving life sentences. To weigh up the arguments for and against their having had a hand in Mills's death, we need an insight into their tastes and temperaments.

The Kray twins, Reggie and Ronnie, were born in 1933. Their lives rotated round Vallance Road, Whitechapel, the area where almost forty years earlier Jack the Ripper had murdered and mutilated four prostitutes. The Krays' manor was the heart of the East End, the nursery of boxers and criminals. In Stepney, Whitechapel, Bow and Aldgate there was no disgrace in having 'been away' (served a prison sentence). On the contrary, it gave a man a certain cachet.

The East End kids were tough. They had to be. Through these back streets and alleys Ted Kid Lewis led his gang of Jewish boys against the

Christian kids, Catholic and Protestant. In these dark yards hidden from view by stalls and pitches, Jack Kid Berg learned how to brawl, so that years later he could match the roughest Bronx tearaway. It was a violent area. In the '60s a tramp was allowed to starve to death within 200 yards of Aldgate Pump. He was no one's responsibility. In the same decade Irish Pat had been sent to prison for committing grievous bodily harm on one of his fellow lodgers at the Spitalfields crypt, which had been opened by the Reverend Dennis Downham as a refuge for meths addicts. When he came out of prison, Irish Pat was met by a delegation of friends of his victim. They held one of his legs in the flames of a bonfire on a bombed-out square until it was so burnt it had to be amputated. It was a practical demonstration of East End justice.

The focus of many of the East End kids used to be the Federation of Boys' Clubs. Annually these boxing kindergartens run their own championships. At the ring-side for these theoretically amateur events can still be found professional boxing managers and touts, for winning a Federation title can be a passport to a successful boxing career and the opportunity of escaping from the East End ghetto. The managers and touts inspect the young boxers as stockmen inspect bullocks at auction. What are they worth? Will they be good 'earners'?

The Kray twins were powerful lightheavyweights. They were physically courageous, and were always fighting, both in and out of the ring. Though they looked exactly alike and shared some characteristics, their tastes and emotions differed. Ronnie was homosexual; Reggie liked women. Both enjoyed violence but whereas Ronnie liked it for its own sake, Reggie thought there should always be a reason for it.

Ronnie enjoyed inflicting pain. To him the most exciting moments of his life were when he committed murder. Reggie employed violence to create fear and so increase the twins' power. Like Jack Spot, he used violence as a business move, as a financier will risk capital if the return is likely to be profitable.

The Kray twins first appeared in court at the age of seventeen. A complaint had been laid that they had razor-slashed and beaten up one of their rivals. Their trial set a pattern: when the case came to be heard, all the prosecution witnesses suddenly suffered from total amnesia. They forgot stories they had remembered earlier when interviewed by police. They contradicted identifications. The magistrates had to dismiss the case.

In the same year that they made their first court appearance the twins became professional boxers. They came from a long line of fighters, their paternal grandfather having been 'Mad' Jimmy, a noted tearaway in his youth, and their maternal grandfather 'Cannonball Southpaw', another famous East End character. However, Cannonball Southpaw fought for the glory of God, not under the influence of the spirits as did Mad Jimmy, who liked taking 'a drop'. The twins' mother, Violet, had been an East End beauty queen, and was a warm-hearted woman much loved by her neighbours. Her sister, however, preserved the family reputation for toughness and had been known to see off female competition with her fists.

Ronnie was heavier than his brother Reggie, who was the brains of the gang which was then becoming widely known as 'The Firm'. But if Reggie planned the operations, Ronnie was the leader who took over as soon as the fighting broke out. Ronnie was known to sit morosely for minutes on end, neither moving nor speaking, but when they went into action he instantly became the commander, issuing orders succinctly and authoritatively. This characteristic earned him the title of the Colonel. He took pride in this nickname and liked nothing better than to have a claque of admiring youths round him as he sharpened his cutlass and armoury of knives, or cleaned his guns. He had no use for razors: he thought you couldn't use enough force with a cut-throat. 'I might be a homosexual, but I'm not a poof.'

In 1952, the twins were called up for National Service. Their army careers were undistinguished, since they spent as much time going AWOL as they did training, and as many months in the glasshouse as in barracks. After two years, the authorities, realizing that there was little if any prospect of turning them into soldiers or worthwhile citizens, discharged them.

Back in the East End they bought a shoddy billiard hall, the Regal. The previous owner accepted £5 for it because he was aware that refusal would probably prove painful. At the Regal, the Krays were kings. It became a magnet for all the East End criminals, and from their 'thrones' beside the tables Reggie and Ronnie arranged burglaries, gang-fights and villainy. They gave sanctuary to thieves on the run from the police. They handled stolen goods, and stored the tools for burglary when the owners were unavoidably detained.

Overtly, the police did not appear interested in what went on in the billiard saloon. No doubt they had their reasons. Perhaps they preferred to leave the Krays alone and to know where the local villains were rather than waste precious hours tracking them. But there were widespread rumours that the Krays had close friends at high level inside the Force.

Certainly, years later, when Nipper Read was in charge of collecting evidence against them, it was claimed by members of The Firm that they always knew exactly what was going on inside the Yard.

By the time they turned thirty the Krays were successful gangsters. All crime interested them. They took on local betting-shops – still illegal then – pubs, cafés, shops and second-hand car-dealers. If the prospective client turned down their offer, they didn't waste time arguing. They went away quietly. But within a few days an accident would happen. The Jaguar in the window of the showroom would be smashed up with mallets during the night. The publican would find his saloon bar had become a regular fight arena and every night something would be damaged in the brawls. Bottles would be broken, upholstery would be ripped. The peace-loving customers would stay away. It was cheaper and easier to employ the twins.

Other gangs withdrew from the territory, or were smashed. To destroy all competition, Ronnie turned his homosexuality to good – or bad – use, organizing a junior gang of boys who acted as his spies and informants. From them he learned where his enemies were drinking, which of them walked home alone at nights, and through which alleyways they went. He found out who was sleeping with whose wife. Then he struck.

However, violence was not the Krays' only stock-in-trade. They acted as go-betweens for thieves and fences and could always find a customer for stolen goods. They advised con-men on areas likely to prove profitable, and suggested people who might be vulnerable to threats or blackmail. This was all business. For pleasure Ronnie always turned to physical brutality.

When a gang from the docks threatened their sovereignty, three dock leaders challenged the Krays to meet them at their local public house beside the river. The dockers were all large, heavily muscled, powerful men. Reggie and Ronnie went alone to meet them. As they entered, the bar emptied except for the reception committee. The landlord retired tactfully to his office. When after an interval he returned, the three dockers were unconscious and he and Reggie had to drag Ronnie away to stop him strangling one of them who looked like regaining his senses. The old adage that bullies are cowards was disproved again and again by the Krays. This victory, in particular, did their reputation no harm.

When Jack Spot turned to the Krays for help on the racecourses against Billy Hill, he must have suspected he was abdicating as king of violence. The twins accepted Spot's offer of a pitch at Epsom, not to help him demonstrate his independence to Hill but because their presence would give notice to all racecourse sharks that the Krays were moving in. For Spot they had nothing but contempt. He was finished, he was the past. They were young and unafraid; they were the present and the future. They admired Billy Hill far more as a quiet operator who protected night-clubs, brothels, gambling clubs and the 'top people'. Hill was a big man, and till then they had only been small fry. Hill was in the big money: indeed, when it came to protection his only rivals were the police.

Though Spot had been a ruthless gang-leader, Ronnie was more than a match for him when it came to violence. At that first meeting at Epsom the Krays made no attempt at secrecy. They *wanted* the underworld to know that they had arrived and were dangerous. Jack Spot had by then had his face slashed in Frith Street, and wanted men working for him who could fight back. He chose the Krays, believing that as fellow East Enders they would be loyal. Strangely, enough, they were . . . for a limited time.

Hill's men left them strictly alone on the Epsom Downs that afternoon. But the Krays had made their point: they had been introduced to the other gangs.

Although the Regal was still Ronnie and Reggie's kingdom, they now had less time to spend in the billiard saloon. They made their headquarters in a club off Tottenham Court Road, close to the Freddie Mills Chinese Restaurant . . . the restaurant which would soon open its doors to the night-club clientele. The Chinese gangs, centred in London's second China Town round Gerrard Street, looked with alarm at this intrusion into their country.

The reason the Krays had been temporarily loyal to Spot was that they needed to draw on his knowledge of the West End rackets. When enemies of Spot caught up with the gang-leader outside his flat in the Bayswater Road, the twins were his first visitors the next day at the hospital, and were fully prepared to avenge him. But Spot remained silent. This last 'cutting' had made him realize that he was growing too old for violence. He had been razored twice within eighteen months. He decided that it was time to retire and go into the furniture business.

Billy Hill also retired, though for different reasons. He had by now amassed enough money to keep him in luxury for the rest of his life. Why should he go on bearing the daily worries and stresses of a successful businessman? He chose Spain for his retirement, thus blazing the trail for so many successful British criminals. He was always a generous host to Reggie and Ronnie when they wanted a holiday.

With the two 'Guvnors' out of the way, the smaller gangs fought for control of the rackets and the territories. The Krays were ambitious, but before they could join in they had to settle a challenge in their own East End, where a gang of Italian immigrants was gaining power. With skilful and ready use of razors, they had been tackling their rivals one by one, beginning with the least powerful and working their way upwards. The twins' informants told them that their names were now next on the Italians' list. Instead of waiting, the Colonel carefully selected the toughest members of the gang, and, informed by one of his boys where the enemy was to be found, conveyed his troops in a van to a social club in the Clerkenwell Road.

Ronnie went in alone. He got a kick out of demonstrating his lack of fear. In the bar, he stopped with a smile as he eyed the amazed group of Italians. He drew a gun and fired three shots in their general direction. No one was wounded, but they were too terrified to counter-attack. Having made his point, the Colonel turned on his heel and walked out without a backward glance over his shoulder.

The Italians wisely decided that an enemy who didn't hesitate to use a gun openly was too much of problem. The Krays' East End kingdom was never again threatened, except by the law.

The three rounds Ronnie had fired – the first he'd ever fired at living targets – damaged only the walls of the social club. The next time he used a gun he hit a docker in the leg, crippling him for life. Ronnie believed, erroneously as it turned out, that the docker had threatened a member of The Firm. Once again there was a police investigation, and Reggie came into his own organizing the cover-up operation. He also made certain that when the docker emerged from hospital, with one leg shorter than the other and no longer able to follow his trade, he was set up for life in a small business. Like everyone else, the victim of the shooting lost his memory as far as the police were concerned.

The shooting set a pattern. Ronnie would act on the spur of the moment, delighting in violence for the erupting release it afforded him. Reggie would then have to pull strings, rehearse witnesses and threaten or coerce those who might have seen what had happened.

It is easily forgotten that the twins brought a strange security to their kingdom. They had their own set of moral rules regarding villainy. Anything was allowed when it came to dealing with rivals or other villains, but the general East Enders were safe. None of the smaller or less important members of the gang mugged old people or beat up the defenceless. In many quarters the twins were popular and respected. Jackie Hopwood, a former featherweight boxer and manager who has a fine sense of humour, told me: 'Boxing was better run by the Krays than it ever was by the Board of Control.'

Again and again they avoided prosecution. Being identical twins also had its advantages. On one occasion, a victim was prepared to identify Ronnie. When the police caught up with the man they believed to be Ronnie Kray, they gave the traditional warning – whereupon Reggie took out his driving-licence and provided a watertight alibi. The police dropped the case.

It seemed nothing could stop the Krays. But Ronnie's uncontrollable temper endangered their safety. When the Krays were told that a new gang, all Irish, was *considering* a take-over, they easily traced them to the pub they used as their headquarters. As the Krays walked in the front door, the Irish challengers disappeared out of the back. Only one man remained, and it is doubtful if he had had anything to do with the plan. He said he'd only stayed behind to finish his pint. Ronnie vented all his frustration on Terry Martin, who was stabbed several times before being kicked into insensibility. He survived, and he talked. Ronnie was arrested, charged, tried and sentenced to three years' imprisonment.

He served the early part of his sentence at Wandsworth. His experience of prison wasn't as harrowing as it usually is for first offenders, since he did not step into an alien world: several members of The Firm were waiting for him as a reception committee. The Krays had always looked after members of their gang who were 'away'; now, in return, they could show their appreciation. Other friends of Ronnie's from the boxing world in Wandsworth also welcomed him. And Reggie meanwhile was working outside on his behalf. He called on the wives of the men serving sentences at the prison, and if their husbands were non-smokers, he'd pay the wives a weekly wage on condition their men passed their tobacco rations over to Ronnie. In prison currency, Ronnie was soon a millionaire.

It was in Wandsworth prison that Ronnie Kray met Frank Mitchell. Mitchell, known as the 'mad axe-man', was a giant physically though a child mentally, and was uncontrollable when angered. Even the prison officers treated him with respect. Mitchell had spent more of his life behind bars than in the outside world, so prison posed no problems for him. He was institutionalized. Ronnie admired Mitchell for his ability to instil fear in others, and they became friends. That was to prove a fatal mistake as far as Frank Mitchell was concerned.

Reggie, worried about the effect prison might have on his brother's already unpredictable mind, realized that, in order to remain at all stable, Ronnie must have something to look forward to, something to dream about. He found the answer in opening a club in Bow Road and, to emphasize the importance it would have for Ronnie when he came out of prison, naming it the Double R.

At the Double R anyone connected with boxing was welcome. Reggie in evening dress would invite the celebrities of the ring to be photographed with him, and always showed off these photographs with pride. There were photographs of him with his arm around the shoulders of Ted Kid Lewis, Terry Spinks, Sonny Liston and Henry Cooper, as well as several with the popular Freddie Mills. This love of boxing and boxers is important for there is a sort of freemasonry among people who box. They respect each other. It would have to be an extraordinary circumstance that induced a boxing enthusiast like Ronnie Kray to harm, let alone kill, a ring hero like Mills. Were there such extraordinary circumstances? It has been whispered that Freddie Mills had turned homosexual. Was his relationship with Mike Holliday a sexual one? Was Kray his rival?

Charlie Kray, the twins' elder brother, a quiet, thoughtful man, joined Reggie and Ronnie at the club. With his stabilizing influence, the Double R flourished and soon they opened a second club next door to the car-park of the Bow Road police station. Reggie again was demonstrating to any doubters that he had nothing to fear from the law.

Ronnie had behaved himself impeccably in Wandsworth prison, wanting to give the authorities no excuse to delay his discharge. In fact, his good behaviour was to work to his disadvantage. Because he was serving a sentence for a first offence and had given no cause for concern, he was transferred to the Isle of Wight, where the prison life was less severe and the Governor and officers were genuinely trying to reform their charges rather than punish them.

But out of London Ronnie's reputation carried no weight. No longer did the inmates fawn on his words, no longer could he buy servants with his extra tobacco. Thrown on to his own resources, he began to brood, and would sit for hours without speaking. The prison officers started watching him carefully. It appeared to Ronnie that everyone had turned against him, and when his family came to visit him, he didn't recognize them – not even Reggie. Being Ronnie, he eventually erupted into violence, was certified insane and moved to Longrove Mental Hospital near Epsom.

In Longrove Hospital he was kept under sedation, and withdrew more and more into himself. He believed that everyone was intent on hitting or maiming him, and in his mind, instead of being the hunter he became the hunted. He sat for hours on end huddled over a radiator. He was diagnosed as being a schizophrenic.

The twins had always been extremely close, so although Reggie was sane he could sense what his brother was suffering. He realized that there was no future for Ronnie until he had served his sentence, and that as long as he was in Longrove his sentence was suspended. Ronnie had to be got out of hospital and back into prison; for preference, back to Wandsworth.

Reggie consulted his lawyers. He studied the Act covering the certification of the mentally insane and learned that if a patient escaped from a mental home and remained at large for six weeks he had to be re-examined before being returned to hospital.

He laid his plans with his usual attention to detail. On visiting day he arrived in the ward wearing a raincoat. When the nurses' attention was elsewhere, Ronnie, dumbly obeying instructions, donned the raincoat and walked out of the hospital into the waiting car. Reggie let Ronnie get well away before identifying himself. While the police searched for him, Ronnie was safely hidden away in a caravan in Suffolk with a powerful ex-boxer as minder.

After the six weeks had elapsed, Ronnie had recovered. He had quickly grown bored with the country life and insisted on visiting the Double R club about which he'd been told so much. Reggie, glad at his interest, threw a party for him after the paying customers had gone home, and from then on it proved almost impossible to keep Ronnie away from the Double R.

But as rapidly as it had recovered, Ronnie's mental health began to deteriorate again. There was no doctor to administer sedatives, and when Ronnie moved back into the family home in Vallance Road, he was once again failing to recognize members of his family, accusing them of being imposters. It was only a matter of time before he would be violent, and the likely victims this time would be his mother, aunt or brothers. Reggie reluctantly called the police. Ronnie walked uncomplainingly to the car when they came to fetch him.

By then, however, Reggie had considerable influence with the police and Ronnie was sent back to Wandsworth to complete his sentence.

With no one left to challenge The Firm in the East End, Reggie now decided to push ahead with their plans for Mayfair, Piccadilly, Shaftesbury Avenue, Chelsea and all the other attractive clubland areas. Reggie and Charlie had by now learned the club business, and became 'minders' of a large club. The club paid them and kept silent. The Krays began taking over. By the time Ronnie came out of prison the brothers were prospering and already becoming well known up West. Far from being gratified, Ronnie resented their new respectability. It was all too peaceful for him. It wasn't 'interesting' – one of his favourite words.

By now a new racket, thriving in the Paddington and Bayswater districts, was one which was to give the English language a new word: Rachmanism. The housing shortage had made people desperate for homes, and desperate people are always vulnerable to the unprincipled. Rachman's tenants were threatened, manhandled and grossly over-charged. If they complained, it was a short cut to physical damage. If Rachman wanted to sell a house, the existing tenants were harassed unmercifully, whether or not they had found any alternative accommo-dation. Rents were raised when and where Rachman wished. If the tenants refused to pay, they were visited by the landlord's agents – large, powerful men. The tenants were often small and elderly. Rachman had no sympathy for non-survivors. He himself had survived Hitler's extermination camps when starving, by eating his own faeces.

Rachmanism provided an interesting new field for the Krays. They made inquiries in Westbourne Park Road and the squares off Portobello Road and Notting Hill Gate. Rachman, informed of their interest, didn't intend allowing any outside gang to disturb the workings of the goldmine he had dug there, but to fight the Krays would be to focus the authorities' attention on his own activities. It was easier and cheaper to find something else to occupy the twins' time – give them a club of their own and they would be too busy to interfere with his activities.

As a result of Rachman's machinations, the Krays found themselves part-owners of Esmeralda's Barn, a profitable gambling club in a mews off Walton St. Among their advisers and associates was a man who became the *éminence grise* in the Krays' more devious, if less violent, operations. Apparently a respectable commuter, he taught them how to make profits without risking losses. He showed them how to form a company and, with comparatively little capital, to create confidence in its financial stability. Once such trust was established, suppliers would be given the largest order they could possibly execute. The day the goods were delivered, the Krays would sell them off at knock-down prices, and by the time the suppliers sent the bill, it would be delivered to an empty warehouse or office.

South of the river, the Richardsons were running a similar operation, but Charlie Richardson didn't need an *éminence grise*. Both he and brother Eddie were intelligent, shrewd businessmen.

Oddly enough the Krays' next clash with the police was not brought about by Ronnie's taste for violence but by an uncharacteristic mistake of Reggie's. A small-time villain was anxious to prove to The Firm that he was qualified to join, and to demonstrate his readiness to take risks he asked Reggie to accompany him when he called on a prospective victim. Unfortunately the victim had anticipated the call and both of them were arrested and charged with obtaining money by threats. Reggie was sentenced to eighteen months' imprisonment.

Without Reggie to restrain him, Ronnie began to lose money at the club. Playing the king, he would grant almost unlimited credit to anyone who approached him sufficiently deferentially. The club manager, a professional, explained that a gambling club accepted a certain proportion of bounced cheques as inevitable, but once this proportion extended beyond an agreed level losses would follow. Ronnie brushed aside the manager's objections. When the warnings proved valid, he flew into an ungovernable rage, and sent his East End strong-arm men to call on those who had issued cheques without sufficient backing. Titled men and women were woken up in the cold hours of the morning by the sound of broken glass as their windows were shattered. Society celebrities, woken by the ring of the telephone, would lift the receiver to hear whispered threats.

The clientele of Esmeralda's Barn, hearing rumours about Ronnie's methods of retrieving debts, had little wish to be connected with it. They wanted no whiff of scandal to attract attention to their recreations, so they took their custom elsewhere. From being a very profitable enterprise which had netted the twins at least £40,000 a year, the club went into the red.

By this time the police had compiled a heavy file on the Krays, but a file cannot in itself prove guilt. When Reggie came out of prison, he learned that a senior officer had ordered that the twins should receive special attention. The subsequent police campaign against them astounded the brothers, who were indignant at what they termed persecution. They were arrested on a host of minor charges, but once again witnesses became forgetful and identifications were doubtful. They were acquitted, and celebrated with a party at Esmeralda's Barn where they posed for the press as they denounced the police vendetta against 'two East End sportsmen who are only trying to make good'. The police would hesitate before trying to put the Krays in the dock again.

British gambling laws have always been illogical. At this time the bookmaker who accepted bets in the street was regularly arrested and fined, and if he had runners they were arrested with their backers paying the fines. But the bookmaker who accepted bets over the phone broke no law. The permissive society sensibly saw no reason why adults shouldn't be entitled to gamble if they wished, and after a major campaign the laws were changed in the early 1960s. Gambling became legal.

Contrary to expectations, this freedom opened wide the doors to even greater abuse. London became the Mecca for European and American gamblers, and the Mafia moved into Mayfair to take an interest in the gambling and night-clubs. They also formulated ambitious plans to fly in gamblers from the States. To carry out these plans they needed a London 'connection' which would have to be powerful and ruthless, prepared to eliminate anyone who stood in the way of the organization. They wanted not only gangsters, but men well known in the West End. The Krays might prove ideal associates for the Mafia, so long as they couldn't be challenged by any other London gang. To attract publicity, they set out to prove they were 'sportsmen', as they had claimed to be during press interviews after being acquitted at the trial, and demonstrated their generosity by running boxing tournaments for charity. Seldom a week passed without a newspaper reporting how Ronnie Kray was giving up his time and money to help unprivileged lads in London's East End.

The twins' influence was now felt throughout the London boxing world. Managers sought their advice and influence. They advised young would-be professionals about which manager was best for them and took a share of promotions. When they opened a new club on the Kingston bypass, they persuaded Sonny Liston, the big bad bear of American boxing, to make a personal appearance there.

The Krays were now more powerful than Billy Hill or Jack Spot had ever been. The only difficulty – as always – was Ronnie's temperament. For weeks on end he would appear normal, but then he would lapse into a depression from which he would erupt into violence. When he had beaten a victim into unconsciousness, Ronnie would recall the details like a gourmet mulling over a *cordon bleu* feast.

One of Ronnie's friends, a young boxer, failing to recognize the symptoms of Ronnie's moods, stopped Ronnie as he went into the bar of a Fulham club and asked for a loan. Usually Ronnie would be flattered by such a request. This time he wasn't. When Ronnie left the club the young boxer was found unconscious on the lavatory floor with half of one cheek lying severed on the tiles beside him.

Ronnie branded his next victim on the face while Reggie pinioned the struggling man's arms.

There was nothing any victim could do. The Krays had challenged the police and won.

But police do not accept defeat meekly. In 1964 Detective Chief Inspector Nipper Read, a former police boxing champion, was attached to West End Central. He spent many hours studying the files on the twins and talking to their victims. But it was usually a one-way conversation. Those who had suffered at the hands of the Krays might hate them, but they feared them too much to grass.

However, one club owner who was not cowed summoned up the courage to go to the police and accuse the twins of demanding a half-share of his profits. Read listened attentively. There was no corroboration for the man's story: the evidence would be mere hearsay and would lead inevitably to another victory for the twins. He decided to wait. The Krays heard of what the club owner had done and a few days later the club was wrecked. But the police arrived there in time to make an arrest, and the man arrested was Mad Teddy Smith, one of the Krays' lieutenants. This was all the corroboration Read needed. The brothers were charged.

They were sent for trial at the Old Bailey, and applied for bail, which was refused. They took their appeal to a higher court without success. But though they might be held in prison, it did not prevent them organizing their defence. As well as engaging top criminal lawyers, they hired private detectives to ferret out everything possible about potential witnesses. As soon as the jury had been selected, the detectives were instructed to investigate those chosen. At that period a verdict had to be unanimous; a majority opinion was not allowable. If only one juror remained unconvinced, the accused would be found not guilty.

The jury failed to reach agreement and there had to be a re-trial. The resulting delay gave the Krays and their private detectives more time. They delved into the past of the club owner who had laid the original complaint, and found he had committed homosexual offences as well as other misdemeanours. At the second trial he was totally discredited. The Krays were once again acquitted.

# 11

THE Krays celebrated their latest victory over the police with a party. From a telephone booth outside the club where the party was being thrown, Nipper Read watched the arrival of the guests. It was a very mixed crowd of stage and film stars, sporting celebrities, businessmen and downright villains. A private detective en route to the party saw Read and recognized him. Unabashed, he invited Read to join him. Read went into the club but did not join the party: from the bar, glass in hand, he watched. He had realized that to bring the brothers to justice he would have to learn every detail of how they lived, who were their friends and what were their weaknesses. A press reporter saw his opportunity – although Read hadn't spoken to Reggie or Ronnie, a photograph taken from a convenient angle would make it appear that they were all together. Critics of the police – and there are always plenty – inferred from the print that Read had been a guest at the celebration.

When, shortly afterwards, Read was transferred elsewhere to concentrate on the Great Train Robbery, Reggie unwisely boasted that he had 'got rid of Read for the price of a glass of champagne'. The fact that Read was promoted *before* his transfer proved that Reggie's claim had no substance. And Nipper Read would be back, as the Krays were going to find to their cost. Having put the Krays away for life sentences, Read would rise in the Force until he was appointed a Commander at the Yard.

When Reggie married an East End girl, many boxers, both old-timers and future champions, were in the congregation. Ted Kid Lewis, the former world champion was present: the wedding was as much a boxing occasion as one for the criminal world. Reggie's wife, a sensitive girl, suffered so severely from the life she was forced to live with him that she eventually committed suicide.

As the Krays were prospering north of the river, south of the Thames another gang was growing in power.

The Richardsons, Charlie and Eddie, had been fated to be criminals. Their father had been born in prison when his mother was serving a stretch, and had served his own sentence for murder. Nevertheless they were very different in character from the Krays. Eddie, a 'traditional villain', ran a successful metal-trading business. Charlie, his elder brother, was a much bigger man in every way: while serving a twenty-five-year stretch in prison, he qualified in psychology, and on completing his sentence became a most successful and respectable company director.

The Richardsons' main source of income came from an activity closely allied to one of the Krays' frauds – the setting up of purchasing companies which would disappear overnight leaving enormous unpaid bills.

Both the Richardson brothers were high-class amateur boxers, and also ran boxing shows for charity. Charlie knew Freddie Mills, but unlike most of the former champion's friends, Charlie is today certain that Mills took his own life, and claims that most of the criminal underworld knew that Mills shot himself because he was going to be arrested for the killing of the Hammersmith prostitutes. This view has been put to me by another notorious villain, who added that, after Mills's death, the police closed the file on the tow-path murders. This view was also repeated to me over the phone by 'Mad Frank' Fraser.

One of those who were in danger from the Krays' gang was a man of mystery, Alan Cooper. Cooper was a cosmopolitan operator who travelled on an American passport. Reggie, at that time, had agreed to distribute a haul of stolen Canadian bonds, and one of the Krays' henchmen suggested that Cooper might prove of assistance. Cooper agreed to handle the deal, part of his commission being that the twins should protect him against any threat from another gang. The Krays accepted this condition.

George Cornell was one of Charlie Richardson's lieutenants, an aggressive and self-confident man brought up in the East End and a one-time friend of the Krays. In a misguided moment, he was heard to refer to Ronnie as 'a fat poof', a sneer that inevitably got back to Ronnie.

The Krays now had three reasons for opening hostilities against the Richardsons. First, they were bound to defend Alan Cooper. Secondly, they should avenge Cornell's insult. But the third reason was far more important: the Mafia negotiations were progressing smoothly, and if agreement with them were reached the Krays would be wealthier than in their wildest dreams. But the Mafia had to be confident that there could be no challenge to the Krays from any rivals. Any competition must therefore be eliminated.

Reggie planned. Ronnie brooded, daily becoming quieter and quieter. He had been grossly insulted, for nothing hurts more bitterly than the truth. George Cornell must be killed, and killed publicly. Ronnie would commit murder so openly that when he was not arrested for it no man would dare work for any other gang but theirs. No one, however strong or famous, would be safe from him.

This theory – that Ronnie wanted to prove he could kill anyone and get away with it – is the basis for some underworld characters' belief that Freddie Mills was murdered. The theory – it has never been proved or disproved – has over the years been embellished with details, which may be accurate or may have been twisted to suit it, and goes like this. 'Mills owned a club. The twins protected clubs. Mills's club was pressured, and Mills would have to pay like everyone else. Rumour had it that Mills owed The Firm £300. If he got away with it, others would follow. A Kray threatener was sent to reason with him. Mills refused to pay. He borrowed a rifle from a friend at Battersea funfair and told friends that if Ronnie Kray came near him he would kill him. His threat was reported back to Ronnie and from that day onwards Mills was watched. The twins learned of Mills's habit of leaving the club at night and taking a short sleep in the back of his car which would be parked in the yard.'

And there, in the yard – according to whispers – Ronnie Kray caught up with Mills and shot him. Mills was famous. Mills was strong. If Mills could be killed with impunity, no one was safe. The Mafia could safely take over London gambling, drugs and crime.

That story is still held to be true by some Soho characters. But there are sound reasons to doubt the legend, as will emerge in due course. Certainly there is no evidence that the club was paying protection-money to anyone. Had they been threatened, Mills and Andy Ho might have appealed to Chinese friends for protection.

What is certain, though, is that at the time of Mills's death London was on the brink of open gang warfare. Life was becoming cheap.

Ronnie was fated to kill, and kill he did. He walked into the bar of the Blind Beggar public house and calmly shot George Cornell through the head. Everyone in the East End knew of the killing and knew who was the murderer. But, strangely enough, no one had the remotest recollection of how it had happened. The barmaid was unable to describe the man who walked into the saloon bar and killed the customer she'd only just finished serving. No customers could recall what exactly had happened: all had been looking the other way.

The Krays were preparing for what seemed an inevitable showdown when their rivals were arrested. A businessman had lodged a complaint, and the police had taken up the trail, which led them to South Africa where a member of the Richardsons' gang, Johnny Bradbury, was under sentence of death for murdering Thomas Waldeck, who had cheated the Richardsons. With his life in jeopardy, Bradbury talked, and had his sentence reduced to imprisonment for life. The Richardson gang was rounded up.

With Charlie Richardson sentenced to twenty-five years and his brother Eddie to fifteen, no one was left to challenge the supremacy of the Krays. The Mafia couldn't fail to be convinced: Ronnie and Reggie were set to become the Godfathers of London.

But now that Ronnie had killed, he had to kill again. Firing that bullet into George Cornell's head, he had experienced an elation which he'd never felt when wielding his fists. Nothing would satisfy him but that Reggie should 'do his' too.

The Krays were never convicted of what was probably their next murder. Frank Mitchell was still in Dartmoor where he enjoyed quite astonishing freedom, being allowed out to visit local public houses and acquiring a mistress whom he enjoyed in the discomfort of Moor Farm outhouses. Why the Krays decided he should be got out of gaol isn't known – one suggestion is that they engineered the escape to impress the Mafia. But they brought Frank Mitchell from the Moors to London and installed him in a flat, where he was provided with drink and even a blond hostess to share his bed.

Mitchell was far from enjoying this. A man who lived on action and excitement, he found the flat as much a cage as his prison cell had been. He threatened to come out and join the Krays, whom he looked on as his saviours, and eventually he became an embarrassment to them. Told he was being moved to a new refuge in the country, he climbed into the back of a van of his own free will. The van drove away. Mitchell was never seen again. The blond hostess kept her mouth shut until everyone else had started talking. Then she told of hearing three short bangs from the street and after that, silence. The flat was cleaned and all fingerprints removed. Frank Mitchell had ceased to exist. That night, it is said, Ronnie Kray cried.

Two other members of the gang also disappeared: Mad Teddy Smith and the youth who had formerly been Ronnie's driver. It was hinted that they'd known too much. Both are still on the list of Missing Persons.

If Mitchell was shot, the trigger certainly wasn't pressed by Reggie.

Reggie had never yet killed, though Ronnie taunted him with being 'soft'. Ronnie had proved himself and was prepared to do so again. Twice he put his automatic pistol to the head of a suspected enemy, but in each instance the automatic failed to go off. On the first occasion, Ronnie calmly extracted the bullet and presented it to his prospective victim as a good-luck token. (Later, when the police were interviewing everyone connected with The Firm, Alan Cooper claimed he had sold Ronnie the gun only after taking the precaution of ensuring that it would not fire. But Cooper was a man of vivid imagination. He also claimed to be an undercover man for the US Treasury and that Scotland Yard would confirm that he was working as an *agent provocateur* to get the Krays convicted. Little reliance may be placed on any of his statements.)

The man chosen as Reggie's murder victim was Jack 'The Hat' McVitie. McVitie was a colourful, violent villain. He drank. He fought. He womanized. He was boastful of his prowess in all three areas, and never tired of telling anyone who'd listen that he was afraid of no man on earth. But after meeting the Krays he began to rely more and more upon pep-pills.

Ronnie hired McVitie to kill Leslie Payne, who – without permission – had decided to withdraw from all the twins' activities. McVitie took the blood-money, bungled the murder attempt, but didn't return the cash. Knowing that the Krays were looking for him, he bought himself a gun. When the Krays were told of the purchase, McVitie was under sentence of death.

Jack the Hat had two close friends, the Lambrianou brothers. Trusting them with his life, he suspected nothing when the Cypriot brothers invited him to a party at Blond Carol's flat. He had no way of knowing that the Cypriots had applied to join The Firm and were eager to prove their reliability to the Krays.

At Blond Carol's flat, Jack the Hat found the twins waiting for him. McVitie proved far from the fearless man he had always proclaimed himself to be. He pleaded abjectly for his life and tried to dive head-first through the window. His hat fell out to the safety of the ground, but its owner was not so fortunate. As Ronnie pinioned McVitie's arms, Reggie stabbed his knife into the victim's face just below the eye. Then he stabbed him again and again before impaling him through his throat to the floor.

Reggie had 'done his one', as his brother had demanded.

McVitie's body vanished. The flat was washed clean, the carpet burned, the furniture removed and Blond Carol was presented with a new suite. Like the axeman Mitchell, Jack the Hat had ceased to exist.

Once again the underworld knew of the murder. Once again no one grassed.

The police knew that London's law and order was being threatened by The Firm, and the twins had to be brought to trial. Nipper Read was called back.

The news that the police were mounting a new campaign against them didn't cost either of the brothers a single sleepless night. They spoke lightly of 'having a friend at court' who would keep them informed of all the police activities. They had outfaced the police twice, and were sure they would do it again.

Read, knowing of the Krays' boast, moved his operation to a small office in Tintagel House, across the river from Scotland Yard, so that no one at police headquarters had access to his plans. Knowing the Krays by now, Read realized that there was only one way to capture and convict them: through their criminal associates and friends.

Before he installed his office at Tintagel House, he spent many hours with the Yard solicitors proposing an agreement such as the pinstripe-trousered gentlemen of the law had never before contemplated. To bring the Krays to justice Read needed to be free to promise all informants that, if they talked, they would *never* be prosecuted for their part in any of the crimes they revealed. The dangers of such legal immunity were obvious, but Read was adamant. This was the only way. He received permission to make the promise.

Read drew up a list of as many victims of the Krays as he could discover and he and his army of twenty men and three women started on the routine foot-work. At first, as was to be expected, no one would talk. The police persevered. They weren't content to make a single visit to each victim; they called back again and again.

When their persistence was reported to the brothers, they began to take the threat more seriously. Reggie remarked that if he were ever again arrested, he knew it would be by 'that clever little bastard, Read'. Ronnie spoke with relish of the more imaginative ways by which he would like to get rid of him.

After eight months of non-stop investigation, Read began to get results. Still no one would agree actually to testify against the brothers, but some made statements that were not to be used until both brothers were safely under lock and key. A clause to this effect was added at the end of every statement and countersigned by Read himself.

The Krays now began to follow the police trail. When a police officer had called on one of the victims, a member of The Firm would follow. They still believed they could frighten their victims into silence, and at first they could. Those who had been party to the Krays' criminal activities were reminded what had happened to other friends who'd stepped out of line – Jack the Hat's name was often mentioned in an aside. Men who'd been shot or beaten up were advised to go to their lawyers and swear affidavits exonerating the Krays. Soon Reggie believed he had blocked every possible loophole.

But one of the men visited by The Firm and given a strict warning was Leslie Payne whom The Firm had sentenced to death before. The Krays' associate since the days of Esmeralda's Barn heard of Jack the Hat's demise and knew that only McVitie's inefficiency had so far saved him. Seeing that his life was in great danger he sent a message to Read saying that he was prepared to tell everything he knew about the twins and their operations.

Read was dubious. He had little reason to trust Payne. But he met him, and every day for more than three weeks the two men talked in the parlour of a small hotel in Marylebone. Payne's final statement ran to over 200 pages.

Read now had the evidence he'd wanted, but he couldn't use it, nor the other statements he and his army had compiled over the months, until the Krays were safely in prison cells. Only then would all the criminals involved turn Queen's Evidence. He would have to bring in the twins on charges sufficiently grave to ensure there was no possible chance of the magistrates' granting bail, and would also have to arrest every other major member of The Firm who, if left free, would silence many of his potential witnesses.

Among the most recent of the Krays' activities was the establishment of an organization based on America's Murder Incorporated. For sufficient money they would kill anyone, to please their Mafia masters. A well-known gambler from Las Vegas staying at the London Hilton had angered the Mafia, who wanted him removed. Though the price offered was only £1,000, the Krays accepted the assignment. Alan Cooper was to be the go-between and he provided the professional killer, Paul Elvey, who was to carry out the contract. Several methods were discussed and even tested but found unsatisfactory. Eventually they decided to blow up the gangster in his car with dynamite.

Elvey, sent to Glasgow to collect the explosive, was arrested. When Read interviewed him, Elvey broke down and confessed. Alan Cooper, invited to Tintagel House for questioning, confirmed Elvey's story but claimed it had all been part of *his*, Cooper's own, plan to trap the Krays and get them convicted.

On 8 May 1968 Read issued his orders: twenty-six members of The Firm were to be arrested as nearly simultaneously as possible. If only one or two got away, or were left free after the others were taken, they might scare witnesses off.

At six o'clock in the morning Read burst into the Krays' home. They were both in bed; Reggie with a club hostess and Ronnie with one of his boys. The twins were handcuffed together before either could offer any resistance.

The charges were mostly minor but were extremely numerous, and were intended to ensure that the twins could be kept in prison while other far more serious charges were formulated from all the statements. But even then there were still difficulties. Two members of The Firm escaped: Ronnie Hart, a cousin of the Krays, and Ian 'Scotch' Brady, who'd been with Ronnie at the Blind Beggar. Read intensified his search for them. Both were caught. Both talked.

With the Krays safely inside, the flood-gates opened. Confession became not only good for the soul but meant impunity from prosecution. Even the twins' closest associates were prepared to grass. Billy Exley, a boxing friend of the Krays and a former bodyguard, was dying. He talked. Former friends went into the box to blacken the Krays and though the defence attacked them ruthlessly their evidence was damning. The barmaid at the Blind Beggar suddenly regained her memory and identified Ronnie as the man who had shot George Cornell.

Ronnie and Reggie were found guilty of the murders of George Cornell and Jack McVitie. The murder of Frank Mitchell, the axe-man, was dismissed, since there was neither a body nor evidence. Many other crimes remained 'on the file', there being little point in extending the longest criminal trial on record when both brothers would be over pensionable age by the time they could pose any new threat to the citizens of London. In March 1969 at the Old Bailey, Mr Justice Melford Stevenson, sentencing them, said that 'in this case *life* should not be less than thirty years'.

In 1981 I visited Charlie Richardson in prison in the Isle of Wight. Reggie Kray was in the same gaol, but there was no enmity between them. Quite the contrary – Charlie introduced me to Reggie and the three of us had tea together, served by a screw.

Whatever the former relationship, today there is mutual respect.

Indeed, when Ronnie Kray remarried in Broadmoor Charlie Richardson was invited as guest. Unfortunately, the Home Office were spoilsports and refused to allow Charlie into the asylum for the criminally insane.

# 12

I N the first twenty-four hours after Mills's death, the police stated in a press release that they were treating it as a case of murder. They had sound reasons for not accepting it as a suicide.

Firstly, the CID had to establish how and where Mills had spent the last few hours of his life. But naturally, with the death of a man so well-known and popular, the press had descended on Goslett Yard and the club like locusts – an ex-world champion found dead in a car in a shadowy cul-de-sac was superb copy. The reporters interviewed anyone and everyone – not only did Andy Ho, Robert Deacon, the doorman, and Henry Grant, the head-waiter, come under their scrutiny, but even the night-club guests who had heard Mrs Mills's screams. This intensive inquisition only served to confuse memories. Answering the same questions again and again as every new reporter arrived led individuals to doubt the details of their own recollections. When someone is told that his memories about time and place do not correspond with the opinions of others who were there, self-doubts creep in. He wavers. He changes his mind. Without the intensive press investigations, the police would doubtless have found it easier to establish an accurate timetable of the dead man's movements.

This initial confusion is clearly demonstrated by the various versions of events published in the press on the Sunday and the following Monday. One newspaper confidently – and exclusively, of course – reported that Mills had arrived at the club shortly after midnight, which left three hours between his arrival and the police being summoned. The time of arrival of the police was variously given as three a.m., three-thirty and four. Another national paper reported that Mills had driven away from Denmark Hill at five o'clock on the Saturday afternoon and had not arrived at the club until eleven-fifty. This, if true, would have left six hours and fifty minutes for which the police would have to account. The crime reporter suggested that this missing period held the solution to the mystery of Mills's death. A third national newspaper reported, equally confidently, that Mills had been seen outside his club at seven in the evening but had then vanished into the twilight, not appearing again until twelve-thirty precisely. This left five and a half hours during which he was missing. A fourth paper suggested that he had arrived at the club early in the evening but that no one had seen him from then until his body was found in his car at one in the morning.

The reports that Mills was seen by several people outside the club before ten-thirty are flatly contradicted not only by Mrs Mills and their daughter, Susan, but by Mrs Budgeon. The three of them stated definitely that Mills had watched the whole of the Morecambe and Wise show on television with his daughters before kissing them goodnight and driving away from Denmark Hill. It would thus have been impossible for him to have been seen at the club before ten-thirty at the earliest.

Further police investigations claimed to show that there were, in fact, no missing hours. Mills had indeed arrived at the club shortly after half-past ten: he had spent no time at someone's flat or at another club drinking. The time element, however, which remains unexplained to this day is how he could have remained slouched in his car for several hours without anyone discovering he was dead and calling the police.

Detective Inspector Virgo of the Yard, who was in charge of the investigation, had also to determine how Mills had acquired a rifle. Mills had never owned any type of gun. Ballistic experts confirmed that the rifle found in the car had fired the bullet which had passed through Mills's right eye and killed him. A second spent bullet, which had gone through the car door, also came from the weapon. The rifle was a Belgian .22 repeater of the type commonly used in amusement arcades. So had Mills bought it surreptitiously in the backyards of Soho, or had it been lent to him by a friend? If he had borrowed it, what excuse had he given? If there were trouble the owner would always be held responsible as he would have to have a licence.

Apparently no one had heard the two shots. Why not? Fairground rifles do not make a great deal of noise but a detective working on the case said: 'In the sound-box of the closed car the first shot must have sounded fantastically loud. It's incredible that he was able to fire again without anyone hearing.'

In using the expression 'sound-box' the detective seems to have accepted that the car doors and windows were all closed. Yet Chrissie Mills's first reaction when getting into the car beside her husband was alarm at his being by an open window when he had recently been ill with pneumonia. Had the detective been wrongly informed, or did someone close the window after Mrs Mills had been taken sobbing into the club?

One reporter, following up the matter of the two gunshots, wrote that waiters at the club, hearing the reports of the shots, had rushed out into Goslett Yard to find Mills dead. This was contradicted by Robert Deacon, a law student who was acting as doorman part-time, who told questioners that he hadn't realized his employer had been shot until the ambulance attendants took the body out of the car.

Yet it *is* surprising that the two shots attracted no attention when Goslett Yard is so very close to the main Charing Cross Road, a busy thoroughfare even late at night. On the other hand, a fairground rifle doesn't have the crack of a service rifle. A shot from a .22 might have been dismissed by a casual passer-by as the back-firing of a car.

The existence of the second bullet-hole in the *front* door of the car was a puzzle – Mills was found sitting in the back. It wouldn't be altogether strange to take a test shot before putting the barrel to one's head, but why on earth would Mills have put such a shot through the bottom of the front car door? It was later surmised that he had begun by sitting in the front of the car and, having taken a test shot close to his feet, might have then got out, walked round to the back, and sat on the nearside rear seat before trying again. If he did make a trial shot, it would seem much more natural that he should have fired out of an open window towards the sky, where the shot could do no damage.

A third bullet, which hadn't been discharged, was found loose on the floor of the car.

The ownership of the rifle was soon established. Mrs Mary Gladys Ronaldson ran a rifle-range at the Battersea funfair. At the inquest, she gave evidence that Freddie Mills had visited her on the Tuesday before his death. His call, apparently, had been social. Casually as he was leaving, he had asked her if he might borrow one of her rifles because he had been invited to open a charity fête dressed as a cowboy. On the Thursday he had returned the rifle explaining that the fête had been cancelled. However on the following day he had come back again and said that the fête had been reconvened and he would like to borrow the rifle again.

When the reporters questioned Mrs Ronaldson about handing over the rifle – a weapon which could kill – she explained that under normal circumstances she would never lend a gun to anyone, but Freddie Mills was a very close friend whom she had known since he had been boxing in a booth close to her shooting-range. Even then she would not have handed over a gun in working condition, but the rifle concerned was faulty, which was why it was in her office when Mills called, instead of being in use on the range. If in fact she told him this, it would support the idea of his taking a trial shot first.

Mrs Ronaldson was adamant that she hadn't given Mills any rounds of ammunition. On being pressed she had admitted that there had been several loose rounds on her mantelpiece and that after Mills had gone, she'd noticed that a few of them were missing.

Mrs Ronaldson recalled that on his last visit, Mills had seemed immersed in his thoughts. As he said goodbye, he'd stood for a moment looking up at the Big Wheel turning overhead. He'd asked her what height it was. When she told him it was eighty feet high, he'd paused for several seconds with his hands on his hips staring upwards.

Although in retailing this anecdote of the day before he died she was implying that he had been contemplating suicide, Mrs Ronaldson said she refused to credit that her old friend could have taken his life. 'I can't believe', she added, 'that he committed suicide. And I can't understand if he did why he left no note. Another peculiar thing is that Freddie told me he was dead scared of guns. He even asked my son to put the rifle into the car for him. He was almost too frightened to touch it. Yet this was the instrument they said he chose to take his own life with.'

When asked what she knew about Mills's financial position Mrs Ronaldson pointed out that the ex-champion had many friends who would have been only too pleased to help him had he been going bankrupt. When pressed to be more explicit she said that she herself was comparatively well-off and would have lent him a substantial sum without the least hesitation.

Chrissie was intensely surprised to learn of this close relationship between her husband and Mrs Ronaldson. Ever since Chrissie and Freddie had been introduced at the Leicester promotion, Mills had taken her everywhere possible with him. If Mills had been such a close friend of the funfair operator, Chrissie would have expected to have met her frequently. Yet, as far as she could remember, Chrissie had met Mrs Ronaldson only once.

Mills might have borrowed the rifle from Mrs Ronaldson with the sole intention of shooting himself. However there is an alternative theory: perhaps he had been paying protection-money for the club to one of the gangs? Since the club was losing money, he might not have been able to find the funds, so the gang concerned might have sent their strong-arm men to 'reason' with him. Mills wouldn't have taken any physical threat supinely, but surely he wouldn't have needed a gun to protect himself against any normal attack? On the other hand, if the gang were known to have killed at least one rival by shooting, then Mills might have borrowed a gun with which to protect himself. Certainly he wasn't the type of man to have fled from trouble. He was an extrovert who'd enjoyed being told how brave he'd been in the ring. He would have been more likely to brag how he had frightened off the threateners than to keep the threats to himself.

In the pubs and clubs of Soho, habitués claimed that Mills had told them in confidence that he had seen off strong-arm villains. Rumour-mongers added that they had heard 'on good authority' that, far from having only a few rounds of ammunition, a week before his death he had bought over a thousand rounds on the Soho black-market. A graphic description also circulated about how he had been seen practising his marksmanship on targets. If there were any substance in this intelligence it raises yet another question: why would Freddie need to practise marksmanship if his only intention was to fire a single shot through his head? And why would he have told Mrs Ronaldson he was so terrified of guns?

Where was the rifle found? One police report said on the front passenger seat; another – which confirmed Chrissie Mills's account – said it was resting against the rear seat; a third said it was between Mills's knees. Two versions were given by the police the day after the death, the third statement was made at the inquest. Why the change?

Chrissie's detailed memory of the discovery that her husband was dead was: 'I pulled myself together. I thought that perhaps he had cut his mouth on the starting-handle. He always kept the handle in the back of the car. It was a fad of his. I thought: "He's dozed off and hit his mouth on it." By this time I'd got my left arm free and I took what I assumed to be the starting-handle and just slewed it across my legs and propped it against the right-hand rear door of the car. Then I turned to put my arms around Freddie again. As I did so the penny dropped. It *wasn't* the starting-handle, it was a gun! Donny, my son, was standing outside the car watching me. I screamed: "It's a gun! Phone the police! An ambulance . . . a doctor . . . It's very bad."'

Reporters were also to write that the gun had been resting between Mills's legs as might have been expected when a man had shot himself through an eye. But a gun expert at the inquest was of the opinion that if Mills had shot himself, the recoil after he had squeezed the trigger would have thrown the rifle sideways, so that it would not have been in any upright position but would have been thrown on to the floor of the car. Chrissie Mills has never deviated from her statement that when she sat beside her husband in the car, Mills was sprawled backwards on the seat, with his knees resting against the back of the front passenger seat. If the rifle had been *between* his legs, she would have had to lift it vertically to free it. In doing so, the muzzle would certainly have jammed against the roof of the car, and she would have had to wrestle it free. She is quite sure that the rifle was resting against the outside of her husband's right leg and that she dislodged it when she moved her left leg against him. To get closer to her husband she had to carry the gun across her own legs, not lift it upwards.

Earlier that night, Mills had been discovered sitting apparently asleep in his car by Robert Deacon, the doorman. Deacon said later that he had first seen Mills arrive about ten-thirty, and Mills had told him: 'I've had a few drinks. I'm going to sleep it off.' Yet according to Chrissie, her husband had left home shortly after ten and he had had nothing alcoholic to drink. If Robert Deacon's estimate of the time is even close to being accurate, Mills would have had no time after leaving home for drinking anything which would need to be 'slept off'.

According to Deacon, the student went out again to the car a short time later. He told reporters: 'At first I thought he was asleep. When he didn't wake up, I thought he'd been taken ill. So I went back into the club and told the head-waiter.' Later the doorman returned to Goslett Yard yet once more and tried to shake Mills awake. This time he had Henry Grant, the head-waiter with him. Grant believes that this must have been a little after one in the morning.

Much later I saw the photographs of Mills taken at the Middlesex Hospital after the ambulance had delivered his body which was certified DOA (Dead on Arrival). Looking at these photographs and seeing how the right side of Mills's face was drenched with blood from his shattered eye, I wondered immediately: Why hadn't those who said they'd tried to waken him noticed the blood? A person doesn't bleed after the heart has stopped pumping, so he must have been blood-stained when they were shaking him. But neither Grant nor Deacon mentioned seeing blood.

Andy Ho claimed he'd telephoned Joggi Villa and left a message for Chrissie only a few moments before she, Donny and his wife arrived at the club. Yet Mrs Budgeon said she'd received the call only a few minutes after they'd left home, and Chrissie Mills is confident she drove up to the door soon after twelve-forty-five.

Although the times are important, considering the delay in sending for the ambulance and informing the police, it isn't wholly surprising that they don't coincide. The doorman, head-waiter and Andy Ho were all busy working, and it is difficult in such circumstances to estimate time exactly. Retrospective opinions are bound to be inaccurate. What can be established is that there was a delay of some three hours between when Robert Deacon claims he first spoke to Mills that night and the ambulance arriving at the club.

Afterwards there was some confusion as to whether or not Mills had made a regular practice of sleeping in his car. At the inquest, the coroner made the point that Mills's going out to sit alone on the back seat of his car in a lonely, dark yard was consistent with a man seeking somewhere remote to end his life. This opinion is logical to anyone not *au fait* with the business of running a night-club.

Chrissie Mills has said that her husband regularly went out to his car for a cat-nap to break up the long evening's work. There was nowhere inside the club he could rest. Indeed, she added that Andy Ho and her husband used to take turns to slip out to their cars for a rest. They worked long, late hours, and needed short breaks from staff and customers, in order to keep alert. The staff of the club confirmed that this was a nightly custom of the partners.

At the time of Mills's death, a small café stood at the corner of Goslett Yard. The café owner recalled that almost every evening Mills used to come out of the club to have a sleep in his car. It had become a stock joke between them. He would shout out: 'Off for your kip, Freddie?' And each night Freddie would find something new and scurrilous to shout back.

The staff who confirmed Mrs Mills's story had, however, a different impression about where he parked his car. They believed he usually parked it not in Goslett Yard but in the main Charing Cross Road. If they were right, then it was an odd choice because the road is widely used, even late into the night. It seemed unlikely he would have been allowed uninterrupted sleep without being woken by the police on their beat, by revellers or drunks.

It also seems odd that Mills would have taken his nightly nap so soon after arriving at the club. Of course, Deacon said Mills had told him he was going to sleep off a few drinks. But at the inquest the Home Office pathologist, Professor Keith Simpson, who said the wound in Mills's head was consistent with 'deliberate self-infliction', also added that Mills had 'a very insignificant amount of alcohol in his blood, which would not have been enough to confuse his thinking'.

Some years later, whilst producing a radio programme about the

Professor, I mentioned that Deacon had reported Mills telling him he was going to 'sleep it off'. The Professor, meticulous as always, looked up his notes. 'He couldn't have had as much as a single measure of spirit,' he told me. Yet Robert Deacon was a law student. He had a trained mind and knew the importance of evidence. Though he might, in all the drama, have been unable to recall Mills's exact words, would he have been likely to misinterpret their meaning?

Andy Ho told the court that Mills was worried about the club losing money. 'Business hasn't been very good,' he said. 'But then it hasn't been very good for any club lately. We don't think this caused it.' When Deacon, the doorman, went out when he drove up on Saturday, Freddie had asked him how many people were in the club. Deacon said: 'Only eight.' Freddie had said: 'Oh, my God!'

# 13

NONE of Freddie Mills's intimate friends admitted noticing any evidence, in recent months, of his being depressed. Mills was an outgoing man who found it difficult to disguise his feelings at the best of times: if he *had* been suffering from acute mental anguish surely at least some of his associates would have noticed his low spirits? They had known about his depressions in the past. Several of his friends told the press of his intense relish for life and his eagerness to be liked. There was evidence, too, that on more than one occasion Mills had openly expressed his contempt for those who had 'taken the coward's way out'.

It was only after his death that it became known that he had unobtrusively worked for the Samaritans, the help-line founded by the Reverend Chad Varah. Mills was no stranger to tragedy. Close friends had died untimely deaths and, as a Samaritan, he had talked with men and women on the verge of taking their lives.

Two years before his death, Mills had invited the actress Ellis Powell to star in his midnight cabaret. 'Lally' Powell was known to millions of listeners as the first Mrs Dale of the radio serial, *Mrs Dale's Diary*. After several years of stardom, the BBC had terminated her contract – a traumatic blow to her self-esteem. From being heard daily on the air and enjoying countrywide fame, she became 'just another actress', one of the eighty-five per cent of Equity members who were likely to be 'resting' at any one time. None of us who met her almost daily in the Stag's Head in Hallam Street had any doubt that her heavy drinking had contributed to the Corporation's decision to drop her from the series. Eventually she had made no attempt to hide her alcohol problem. Although he must have known this, Freddie Mills had decided he would try and help her out of her desperation.

When, in May 1963, Mills suggested to Lally Powell that she should star at his Nite Spot, she grasped at the opportunity. Friends who had watched her degeneration believed Mills was genuinely saving her life. It wasn't to be. Perhaps Lally found herself terrified to step again into the spotlight: appearing in cabaret before a live audience is vastly different from the informal atmosphere of a recording studio. Perhaps she realized that this type of work was now beyond her. Whatever her fears, they proved too much for her. A week before she was to open at the Nite Spot she was found unconscious at her flat, and later died in hospital. The cause of death was given on the Death Certificate as 'cerebral haemorrhage', but most of us believed it should have read 'a broken heart'. Lally Powell's death illustrated how difficult it is to become an unknown after having enjoyed national fame. Maybe her death fanned fears in Freddie's mind? He was keenly upset by it.

He was just as crushed at the suicide of Michael Holliday, the singer. Holliday was one of Mills's closest friends; indeed, many have since hinted that their friendship was 'unnatural'. Certainly there was a close rapport between the ex-boxer and the ballad-singer. Apart from friendship, Mills had a genuine admiration for Holliday's theatrical personality and polished professionalism. The singer had enjoyed a spectacular success in the very field Mills had chosen when hanging up his gloves. Mills, though almost over-confident on the stage, had no undue opinion of his own voice, and envied Holliday's purity of tone. However, this envy was expressed openly and the singer could have had no better publicist. There was no worm of envy eroding Mills's confidence.

Holliday suffered from acute depression, his moods switchbacking from over-enthusiasm to bitter moroseness. Mills and Chrissie, realizing Holliday's frequent feelings of resentment, tried to enfold him with the love and security he needed. Again and again they insisted he come to the night-club as their guest. On his last visit they prevailed on him to sing, hoping that the applause of the guests might turn his thoughts outwards instead of towards his sense of helplessness.

Holliday sang 'I Can't Believe That You're In Love With Me', and as the audience clapped enthusiastically, he stood silent, almost unmoving, gazing out into the smoke-filled distance as if he were deaf to the noise. When he went back to his table and his hosts, he told Chrissie and Freddie that he wished he were dead. Mills remonstrated: 'You're talking balls, chum, sheer utter balls. You must live out life to the end. Life's exciting. Life's great! Nothing can excuse anyone trying to "end it all".' The other guests at the table never forgot Mills's words.

The day after Michael Holliday had sung at the Freddie Mills Nite Spot, he was found in a coma from which he never regained consciousness. It was a real tragedy because after some difficult times he was again enjoying stardom and had a spectacular future before him. Nevertheless, it wasn't entirely unexpected. There was no doubt that he was a manic-depressive.

After Mills's death, his close friends recalled how he had felt himself a part of Holliday's misery; almost as if he were partly responsible for it. No doubt this emotion helped to fan the rumours that their relationship had been of a homosexual nature, and tittle-tattlers drooled over the suggestion that Mills had thought he was about to be arrested for homosexual activities. But no one – family, friends, casual acquaintances or fans – ever saw Freddie Mills displaying symptoms of severe mental disorder.

Only a few days before his death in Goslett Yard, Mills had sat in Frank Duffet's office and told his former trainer that he realized he had made many mistakes since retiring from the ring. Now he had come to the conclusion that night-club life was not for him. Duffet recalls that Mills, having made up his mind on this point, was enthusiastically formulating new plans. He was talking excitedly of promoting on a much larger scale, seeing many opportunities for himself in the boxing world. This enthusiasm sits strangely with a man contemplating suicide in the immediate future.

Without any attempt to hide the truth, Chrissie Mills says that she and her husband had on several occasions experienced financial difficulties. Far from allowing such problems to prey on his mind, she says that Mills was almost too ready to brush them aside. She had had to persuade him to face up to facts. He had always countered her predictions of doom by pointing out that they had capital behind them in the form of the property Bill Bavin had bought on his behalf. He had earned thousands of pounds with his fists – what if he did lose a few hundred on the club? If the losses became more than they could afford they would sell the properties. Chrissie Mills believed fervently that her husband would never have committed suicide because of shortage of cash. There was more than a little touch of Mr Micawber in him.

The idea that he would have committed suicide because of possible prosecution for breaking the licensing laws is risible. The members of the Freddie Mills Nite Spot would have been more amused than shocked by such a prosecution. As for the call-girl story, Mills certainly wouldn't have been shocked if he had thought a member of the staff was organizing prostitution from the premises. He had friends who were film-stars, gamblers, gangsters, ponces and policemen. He had come into close contact with society women who looked on professional boxers as scalps to be hung from their suspender belts. He numbered amongst his admirers call-girls who would, if brought to court, term themselves models; and whores who would claim to be chorus girls (there was a popular joke at the time that a chorus girl was one who earned £4 a week and sent £6 a week home to mother). He had signed autographs for fourteen- and fifteen-year-olds who competed to see who could bed the greatest number of popstars. He had served in the forces and had travelled overseas. He would hardly have held up his hands in horror to learn that his hostesses augmented their tips after hours by 'doing a turn'. Mills might not have enjoyed this aspect of club life, but it was a fact he must have accepted when he decided to transform the Freddie Mills Chinese Restaurant into the Freddie Mills Nite Spot.

He was more likely to have been hurt by the decision that had been taken to change the name of the ailing club to the Marrakesch. He had been so very proud of everyone hearing about his club, and enjoyed welcoming the guests with, 'I'm Freddie Mills and this is my club.' It wouldn't be the same to say: 'Welcome to the Marrakesch.' But would he have killed himself because of it?

Of course the old cliché *Cherchez la femme* wasn't allowed to remain unspoken. There is not the slightest suggestion that Mills flirted with, let alone bedded, any other woman after he married Chrissie. If he had wished to stray, he was surrounded by many attractive women who would have been only too ready to accede to his wishes, but he would never have allowed this to endanger his happiness with Chrissie, or his family life.

However his apparent faithfulness to Chrissie failed to muffle the scandalmongers, who managed to dredge up a whisper that whetted the appetite of everyone who heard it. Prostitutes in Hammersmith had been found murdered and mutilated by the tow-path. It is possible that the suggestion that Freddie Mills was the murderer was dreamed up by those who wished to conceal the fact that he had been killed by a London gang – at any rate, it was rumoured that the hounds of the law were closing in on him and that, rather than stand in the Number One Court of the Old Bailey facing a charge of murder, he had preferred to take his own life. This rumour still persists today, especially amongst ex-cons. Villains have whispered to me: 'Freddie was responsible for those tarts' deaths. After he topped himself the police closed their files on the murders. They wouldn't have done that if Freddie had been innocent, would they?'

Certainly it is true that no one has been arrested for these murders. But the police would never close a file on a murder without anyone being charged. If they had done so after the death of Mills, it would have been to find him guilty without trial. At the same time, the rumour has persisted so it must be considered.

What about the theory that he killed himself in a fit of inexplicable depression? The late Dr William Sargant, author of *Battle for the Mind*, and a very eminent psychiatrist, said that depression is the most painful of all conditions, and Andy Ho, at the inquest, told the coroner that Mills had indeed suffered from severe depressions. On the other hand, Chrissie Mills denied it emphatically. 'In twenty years you get to know a person. You know his moods. But never, never did I see Freddie sink into the depths. Besides, Freddie was a fighter. He wouldn't have let me or the kids want for anything. I'm sure that even if the club was doing badly, it wouldn't have weighed him down . . . but he did want to get out of the club, there's no doubt about that. He realized it had been a mistake. We just weren't night-club people.'

Chrissie Mills, like many others, considered the absence of any suicide note of great significance: 'Freddie had an extremely close affinity with our elder daughter, Susan. If he hadn't left a note for me or the coroner, he would still have had to give *her* an explanation.'

Frank Duffet is another who will never believe the coroner's verdict was correct. Although their joint promotions hadn't made them a fortune, Duffet claims Mills hadn't lost money on them. He said: 'If he'd lost on our promotions, he wouldn't have been so keen to start up again indoors at Bristol. We were already planning to open again as soon as we'd found a suitable arena.'

Duffet had a detailed and clear memory of Mills's last visit to him. 'It was roughly a week before his death. He came to my place in Waterloo and sat down. He had a cup of tea. Then he began to talk to me. He said he'd been a chump in the past and that he'd made mistakes . . . though he didn't go into what they were. I said: "Well, you're not the only one, mate." Then he gave me the impression he was back on an even keel and was looking forward to the future and starting something else.'

Years later Frank Duffet ran into an old acquaintance who had seen Mills on the very afternoon of the day he died. 'This man', Duffet said, 'ran an off-licence close to Denmark Hill. Every Saturday Mills used to go in to buy his weekly supply of cigarettes. The licensee has since emigrated to Canada and was on a visit home when I met him.

'He told me that on the Saturday of his death Mills came into the off-licence about five-thirty. There were several people in the shop and, as usual, Freddie started to fool around to entertain them. He sparred up the owner saying: "I'll take you any time . . .", then he pretended to take a wild swipe at the licensee before collapsing with laughter. The off-licence owner believed that Freddie was acting like a man who was "in love with life". He said to me: "I'll never believe he committed suicide a few hours later. I'll never accept it."'

Others who knew Mills far better than that licensee also refused to believe that so courageous a fighter would kill himself because of financial troubles. Jack Solomons told me: 'Freddie never gave the impression he would ever commit suicide, Tony. He had the guts to face anything in the world.' On the other hand, leading promoters today, Mickey Duff, Solomons' original match-maker, and his partner Jarvis Astair, both believe Mills took his own life.

Solomons believed that Mills's rocky finances – which would come to light after his death – had two causes. First, the ex-boxer had poured far too much money into the ill-fated night-club venture. Second, he had been far too generous. 'Freddie was an easy touch. He only had to meet someone in the street who spun him a hard-luck story and Freddie would be tapped for £25, £50 or £100. He couldn't help it.'

Jack Solomons, who had heard most of the rumours as to why Freddie Mills might have killed himself, or been killed, didn't for a minute believe the answer was to be found in the protection-racket story. 'Freddie was never afraid of anybody. I don't think any protection fellows would have dared to go near him. Freddie would have faced them and told them what to do and where to go.'

The late Teddy Waltham, former general secretary of the BBBC and the referee who had raised Mills's hand at the end of his world-championship victory, took a similar view. He could not believe that so brave a fighter would ever have taken his own life. Nor did sportswriter Gilbert Odd, one of Mills's oldest friends, who said: 'Suicide is to an extent a cowardly way out of trouble. Nobody on earth could call Freddie a coward. His mere record shows he always took on great odds.'


You have decided to kill yourself. It isn't a decision taken out of desperation on the spur of the moment: that's shown by the fact you have previously gone to a funfair to borrow a gun, but then you have returned it. That might be the action of a man whose resolution has faltered, who finds he hasn't the courage to put a bullet into his eye – or, again, it could be that of a man whose circumstances have suddenly changed dramatically for the better.

Now, perhaps, circumstances have changed again, or desperation has overwhelmed you once more. You've borrowed the gun again, from a friend who is bound to be alerted by your doing so for she knows of your lifetime hatred of such weapons.

You will probably be able to hide the rifle in your car, but can you conceal your feelings from everybody you meet, as well as those who are dearest to you? After your death many motives for your taking your life will be suggested, but none of them can account for how you managed to appear so calm, happy and content whilst you ticked off the minutes till you pressed the trigger.

If you had been going bankrupt surely you would not have just given up, especially with your reputation for guts? At least you'd have announced a boxing come-back, which would have earned you time. Besides, you have a row of houses you have bought: you could sell them. Your pride might prevent your going round your friends seeking a hand-out, but surely you would ask the advice of Jack Solomons before you did anything desperate? You made Jack Solomons thousands of pounds and he's always pressed you to go to him for help whenever you need it – his reputation would suffer if he didn't help you. Frank Duffet, your friend and co-promoter, ought to have known how worried you were, but Duffet had no hint of your intention to kill yourself. Not even your wife Chrissie knew you were so concerned. She had been brought up in the boxing world and had seen millionaires go bankrupt overnight. She would have backed you in whatever you had to do to get straight again.

If the night-club were doing badly, you would have had no difficulty selling it, with the current boom in night-life. And if you were being threatened by gangsters, surely your reaction would have been to fight back rather than remove yourself from their way? Besides, you know all the major gangsters: they are your friends. If one particular gangster hated you because of some imagined slight or because you had stolen his boyfriend you could surely have gone to his brother? Or, if that were impossible, you could have demanded protection from the police – several high-ranking officers were regulars at your club. But whatever the reason, if you were threatened, wouldn't you have shared your fears with Andy Ho, your partner, who would also have been at risk?

If you had feared bad publicity because you were going to be prosecuted on account of hostesses using the club as a centre for a call-girl racket, why didn't you discuss it with Chrissie? She knew the night-club game and that most hostesses augmented their meagre wages by working after hours. She wouldn't have been shocked. She was a woman of the world.

If you were about to be arrested for homosexual activities, as has been widely suggested, you probably wouldn't have been able to tell Chrissie of your fears: that might have been a reason to keep your planned self-destruction to yourself. And if, as is believed by many in the criminal fraternity, you had killed several prostitutes, you certainly wouldn't have shared the facts with any other person.

But whatever your motive for killing yourself, would you have been able to spend the whole day with your wife, and much-loved children, your friends, partner and club staff, without a single one of them noticing anything untoward in your behaviour? To do so you would have had to be the most consummate of actors . . . and that you certainly weren't.

# 14

O N 30 July 1965, Frederick Percival Mills was buried at Honor
Oak Cemetery after a service at St Giles's Church in Camberwell. The internment was intended to be private, but Freddie
Mills was too popular and – by now – too theatrical a figure to make his
last exit without an audience. Men, women and children of all classes,
races and colours wanted to pay their last respects to the former
lightheavyweight champion of the world . . . or just wanted to 'get in on
the act'.

In the pews of the Camberwell Parish Church television personalities
sat shoulder to shoulder with local tradesmen and publicans. Former
booth-boxers hitch-hiked from the West Country to pay their tribute to
one of their own. Some of Mills's undoubted glamour had been shed on
their rough, uncompromising trade. Local bookies in unaccustomedly
sober suits whispered discreetly to models from the High Street dress-
shops, whose cleavages were far higher than usual out of respect for the
occasion. Everyone there would have claimed a personal friendship with
the deceased.

More than a thousand crammed into the church whilst at least another
thousand stood outside, straining to identify all the celebrities.

One group inside the church, chatting amongst themselves, were
unrecognized by the crowds – social workers from South London had
come to say their farewells. They knew Mills not only as the extrovert ex-
boxer but as a colleague from the Camberwell branch of the Samaritans.

The Reverend John Nicholls, the vicar of St Giles, told his
unaccustomedly large congregation: 'Freddie used to spend a night every
week at the vicarage discussing personal problems with anyone who
cared to come. He saw alcoholics, drug-addicts, in fact, anyone in
distress. He helped talk people *out of* suicide.'

At the word 'suicide', many of the congregation exchanged glances.

That very morning one national paper had carried the story that Mills had been heard to say he could not understand anyone taking his own life. A show-girl friend had told reporters: 'He was severely affected emotionally by the sudden death of Michael Holliday and blamed himself for not preventing the singer's suicide. He told me: "I can't understand anyone wanting to take his own life. Life is far too good."'

In some aspects life *had* been good to Freddie Mills. From modest beginnings as the son of a rag-and-bone merchant, he had fought his way to world fame. From running behind a milk-dray through the back streets of Bournemouth, he had become a theatre, television and radio personality. From appearing at a juvenile court accused of stealing a pair of skates, he had graduated to giving a boxing exhibition at Buckingham Palace. Could a man with such a dramatic career behind him, and so much to look forward to, have become so desperate that he borrowed a fairground rifle and fired a bullet into his eye?

The pall-bearers, all close friends, were organized by Jack Solomons. With him were Teddy Waltham, representing the BBBC, and Johnny Williams who had featured with Mills at the Buckingham Palace performance. Peter Wilson, undoubtedly the greatest boxing writer since William Hazlitt, was another pall-bearer, as was Bruce Forsyth, the TV personality, who gave the address, saying: 'To be loved in sport and showbiz – two very tough professions – is a very rare thing indeed.' More than sixty wreaths were on or in the hearse and the cars following the cortège. A card with the one word 'Broken' was pinned to a heart-shaped wreath of red roses; it was Chrissie and her two daughters' farewell to a husband and father. Another card, almost as brief, read: 'Freddie Mills – the Champion from Jack Solomons'.

A week after the earth had been shovelled back over the coffin, the mourners, who had stood with bowed heads at the graveside, were thunderstruck to learn that the Westminster coroner had announced: 'I have no doubt that it was a deliberate action. Mills died from a firearm wound to the head. This was self-inflicted, and so he killed himself.'

While giving evidence at the inquest. Chrissie Mills had broken down in tears. When asked about her husband's moods at the time of his death, she told the coroner: 'He was in great form but had been quieter than usual for a few days. He hadn't fully recovered from a virus infection and seemed a bit worried about business and bad publicity.' So Mills had not been afraid to discuss the hostess affair with his wife, and had been able to share his worries with her. He had had no cause to feel alone and isolated.

Andy Ho had also spoken of their business problems and of Mills being depressed. Professor Keith Simpson, who had carried out the post-mortem, stated that the wound in Mills's head was 'consistent with deliberate self-infliction'. He had, of course, also examined the contents of the stomach. 'There was an insignificant amount of alcohol. Certainly not enough to confuse his thinking.'

So the verdict was that Freddie Mills, ex-champion of the world, had killed himself. The coroner did not pursue the apparent incongruities, let alone the contradictions in the evidence.

To recap: Mills, according to Robert Deacon, had said: 'I have had a few drinks and I'm going to sleep it off.' With whom and where had he had those few drinks? Why did he want a nap when he had only just arrived at the club and had only a few hours earlier enjoyed a siesta? If he had been drinking, as he said, why was there so little alcohol in his stomach?

Why were there such extraordinary discrepancies of time? If Robert Deacon and Henry Grant were accurate in their memories of that night, then Chrissie Mills was wrong. Yet Susan and Mrs Budgeon could confirm her estimates as to her husband's movements.

The coroner considered that Mills's going out to his car in Goslett Yard was consistent with the actions of a man seeking a suitable private place to kill himself. Disagreeing with this hypothesis, Mrs Mills declared that her husband used to sleep in his car almost every evening when he was working at the club. The proprietor and regulars at the café which stood at the corner of the yard could have confirmed her assertion. But they were never questioned. The night-club staff could also have said that Mills and Ho went out each night in turn to sleep in their cars. They were not questioned about this at the inquest, either. However, they claimed to the press that Mills usually parked in the main Charing Cross Road rather than by the back door of the club in Goslett Yard.

Chrissie Mills was not asked at the inquest whether she had moved the rifle in the back of the car. Nor was Donny McCorkindale questioned, although he too had touched the rifle when trying to help his mother out of the car when she had realized her husband was dead.

At the time of the inquest, the coroner would not allow the press to read the record he had made or to see the photographs of the body taken at the hospital. This is a decision entirely within the coroner's discretion. However, after a passage of more than twenty years, his successor generously gave me permission to read the whole report and to see the photographs, which clearly show Mills's face covered in blood. The omission of any questioning of those who could have thrown so much light on what had transpired that evening is quite remarkable.

A leading psychiatrist, having studied reports on Mills's character, told the *Daily Mirror*: 'It is my experience that only a person committing suicide on impulse doesn't leave a note. I would certainly expect a note in a premeditated suicide by a man like Freddie Mills, who was an extrovert.'

The coroner thought the fact that Mills borrowed, returned and borrowed again the rifle from Mrs Ronaldson was a clear indication of premeditation. But if it was premeditated, why did the ex-champion leave no note? Apart from wanting to tell his family why he'd taken his life, surely he would have wished to clear Mrs Ronaldson of blame for having lent him a dangerous weapon? After all, she had broken the law by doing so.

The coroner was apparently not interested in the position of the rifle in the car. The *Daily Mirror* made a special feature of this aspect of the case. Ronald Maxwell, one of their most experienced reporters, called in Leonard John Pearce, the managing director of Churchill (Gunmakers) Ltd. Mr Pearce, a ballistics authority, had frequently been consulted by Scotland Yard over firearm cases. The reporter and the firearm expert carried out their own experiments in the Citroën with Donny McCorkindale playing the role of his late stepfather. Chrissie arranged her son's hands as her husband's had been when she'd got into the back of the car beside him: unclenched and resting on his knees. She also placed the rifle in the position in which she'd found it before she'd picked it up and carried it across her body.

Mr Pearce, though professionally cautious, decided nevertheless that there were several incongruities.

Chrissie and her son agreed that Mills had been sitting on the nearside rear seat of the car. Before Chrissie had moved the rifle that night, it had been resting upright against the outside of her husband's right leg, *not* between his legs as one police report had claimed. Medical evidence had shown that Mills would have died almost instantaneously from the shot through his right eye. Mr Pearce could find no way of firing the rifle so that it could come to rest by itself as Mrs Mills had found it.

In the *Sunday Mirror*, Maxwell summed up Mr Pearce's findings: 'We found that the gun, hands and wound would only be in the correct position if the rifle were fired through the wide-open window.'

Another point which surely demanded an explanation was how and why the second shot had been fired at all? This shot had passed through the bottom of the nearside front door of the car. The *Sunday Mirror* offered three possible answers.

One, the shot could have been fired during a struggle. But Mills would have been unlikely to lose a fight in an enclosed area. Surely he would have had to be knocked unconscious before the assailant could step back, aim and fire a shot into the ex-boxer's eye? Yet the post-mortem had revealed no damage to his body. There was no mention of bruises or abrasions.

Two, Mills could have fired the shot himself, to test the rifle and make certain it would work when he put it to his head. Certainly, Mrs Ronaldson might have mentioned that the gun was faulty when she'd handed it over. Yet surely a man sitting in his car, contemplating killing himself, would be more likely to fire a testing round through the open window than into a door close to his feet? Death can be less frightening at the last moment than the possibility of painful injury. Furthermore, such a shot within the car would reverberate and so could have been heard by a casual passer-by, in which case he would probably have been disturbed before he could fire a second shot.

Three, Mills could have been shot through the window of his car by someone who hadn't realized the rifle was a repeater. The killer could easily have discharged the round inadvertently when reaching inside the car to place the weapon beside Mills's body to suggest suicide. The rifle, being faulty, might well have been triggered off by a casual rap on the butt. Not being tightly held, it might well have canted over the front seat so the bullet drove wildly into the front door of the car. If this were so, the loose shot would have been fired after Mills's death, not before.

On the Sunday that the *Sunday Mirror* published its deduction, ghoulish sightseers picnicked on Mills's grave, stripping it of the dying flowers, decaying wreaths and clay-soiled cards. No doubt these relics would be treasured souvenirs of a happy day's outing.

Two evenings later, the Freddie Mills Nite Spot reopened after a two weeks' closure out of respect to its former owner. The drama and publicity over Mills's death might have attracted scavengers to his graveside but they hadn't drawn club guests. Business was no better than it had been on the last two nights before his death, and after four evenings of meagre takings and muffled talk, the club doors were finally closed.

In a matter of twenty days, Mills had died, been officially declared a suicide, and been buried. His grave had been desecrated and his night-club closed. It could have been the last act in 'The Life and Death of Freddie Mills'.

It wasn't – although for the next three months it appeared the final curtain had fallen.

Chrissie Mills had resolutely refused to accept the coroner's verdict, and by November she was hearing strange rumours from the back alleys of Soho. They provided the stimulus for her to investigate further. On Donny's advice, she hired a private detective.

In late November, a reporter scooped the rest of Fleet Street with a dramatic story. Donny McCorkindale in an exclusive interview was reported as saying: 'My mother and I have never thought Freddie killed himself. Now we have enough information not only to assure us he did not kill himself but also to convince us we know who *did* kill him. A private prosecution, I understand, is the only course open to us. The police told us after the inquest that we would find it extremely difficult to have the suicide verdict changed. They said that if we managed it, it would certainly act as a precedent. Now a lawyer has told us that our best course would be to start a private prosecution.'

Mrs Mills had employed a private detective to investigate the last hours of her husband's life. Private detectives are very expensive and she had very little money. How could she afford to fund further enquiries?

Donny McCorkindale was active in the entertainment world and had many friends among singers and disc-jockeys. Chrissie turned to them for help. They all claimed to have been personal friends of her husband and many of them were wealthy. As they worked in clubs and discos, they could also ask questions and keep their ears to the ground. They posed the questions suggested by Donny and reported back that as soon as they mentioned Mills's name to any of the shadier characters, a strange hush descended.

Three months after Mills's death, his widow received a mysterious visit. As Chrissie was collecting her car from the garage in front of Joggi Villa, a man came into the garden and up the drive. Politely he asked if she were Mrs Mills. 'The wife of Freddie Mills?'

'The widow,' Chrissie replied.

He stood stock-still for several seconds looking directly into her eyes as if wanting to impress her with the importance of what he was going to say.

'Please don't waste any more time or money on private detectives. You can't afford it. Besides, it wouldn't please people who have an interest in the case.'

Without another word he turned on his heel and walked back on to Denmark Hill.

Chrissie Mills, a woman of considerable determination and courage, decided to ignore this threat.

Clarifying the exact financial position of a dead man who worked in so many diverse fields can be time-consuming, especially when death is sudden and unexpected. Long before the final account of Freddie Mills's affairs had been agreed, it was evident that although his wife could keep Joggi Villa, she and her daughters would have little or no capital left.

Freddie had appeared so often on charity shows for others without any payment that it was only just that his former showbiz friends should now come to the help of his widow and daughters. On 6 February 1966, Mrs Mills and Susan and Mandy were the centre of attention in the audience at the Prince of Wales Theatre for 'The Freddie Mills Night'.

This posthumous charity performance was sponsored by his former friends and admirers. Among those who gave their services were Tommy Trinder, Norman Vaughan, Eric Sykes, Hattie Jacques, Bud Flanagan, Peter Murray, Ted Ray, Harry H. Corbett and Tommy Cooper. They all knew Mills personally, and none of them could accept that the convivial, brave man they'd known and been proud to call friend would have taken his own life.

The accounts for the show were still being audited when the details of Mills's estate were published. The ex-champion who had earned so much money in the ring, on the stage and as a promoter left only £387.

Not even those closest to Mills could suggest an explanation. Where had the money gone? What had happened to all the property bought against that 'rainy day'? His father-in-law, Ted Broadribb, told the press: 'I took Freddie over when he was a £25-a-bout fighter. In the next seven years he made more than £100,000 gross. I cannot say how much was net.' (Few managers like to reveal exactly how much has been siphoned off purses by the time they reach the boxer.) 'I freed him from the last year of his contract and he made a great deal of money from writing, public appearances and as an entertainer.'

Jack Solomons had paid Mills most of the £100,000 mentioned by the manager. From his office in Windmill Street, the promoter commented: 'Freddie was too proud to tell anyone the club wasn't doing well. But *that* is where most of his money went.'

In the last three years of his fighting career, having made that £100,000, Mills had earned at least another £70,000 which included the £11,000 he had received for his losing contest with Joey Maxim. Could all his purses, plus his fees for radio, films, television, cabaret and personal appearances, have been consumed by his Nite Spot losses? He was, as Jack Solomons had pointed out, an easy pavement touch, but were there other outgoings, of which no one knew?

It has never been established where Mills's money went – whether he had hidden expenses, or whether others had exploited him or cheated him.

# 15

THE rumours that Mills had been the victim of a gangland execution persisted. But the police deal with facts not whispers, and the coroner had given his verdict, so the police investigations were brought to an end.

Two years elapsed before Freddie Mills again made headlines, during which time Chrissie Mills never ceased badgering the police to reopen the case. Meanwhile she had to live extremely prudently for, despite the proceeds of 'The Freddie Mills Night', she had had to take part-time work so that she and her daughters could continue to live at Joggi Villa. She knew the police weren't satisfied that her husband had committed suicide, and believed that – like herself – they really thought he had been murdered. Accepting that their hands were shackled by the coroner's verdict, she told me that she'd been informed in confidence by several very senior officers that eventually the Yard would be forced to listen to her. Daily she expected to hear that the Commissioner of the Metropolitan Police had ordered the case to be reopened. Her expectations remained unfulfilled.

Chrissie Mills was delighted when in March 1966 the Freddie Mills Club for handicapped children was opened in Vauxhall. It reassured her that her husband was not forgotten. In the same year she unveiled a black marble memorial stone, paid for by individual contributions of boxing followers, at the head of his grave. On the centre of the grave was a white stone boxing glove which was, in fact, an urn containing one of Mills's gloves wrapped in plastic for preservation.

In the two years after his death, the London underworld heard of the murders of Frank Mitchell, 'Jack the Hat' McVitie and George Cornell. Most of the metropolitan criminals had been well aware of the activities of the Kray twins; relatively few, however, had known of their negotiations with the Mafia. Confirmation of the fact that the Krays were able to kill openly loosened many tongues and started speculation.

If gangsters as well known to the underworld as McVitie and Cornell could be executed with impunity, might not Freddie Mills have been another victim of the twins? Had he offended them in any way? Had he spoken derogatorily of Ronnie or incurred his jealousy? Had the Krays wanted to demonstrate to possible future partners that they could kill anyone, however famous? Had Mills stood up to them and had to be eliminated if only *pour encourager les autres*?

On 8 May 1968 Nipper Read arrested Ronnie and Reggie Kray in the early hours of the morning, and from then on the denizens of the sewers felt free to talk. Chrissie Mills, reading of the arrest of the Kray brothers, wondered again about the identity of the sinister stranger who had called at Joggi Villa, and of the 'people who have an interest in the case'.

She had additional reasons for suspecting that gangsters – if not the Krays – might have been responsible for her husband's death. Her son Donny had emigrated to South Africa, his father's homeland, and there had received an invitation from a man in prison. This prisoner, serving a life-sentence, had claimed that he knew how and why Freddie Mills had been murdered. He was only prepared to give this vital evidence to the dead man's stepson.

This tale was later followed up by Bill Bavin and described in detail in his book *The Strange Death of Freddie Mills*.

Johnny Bradbury, known in South Africa as John Lawrence, was a London mobster from the East End who had known the Krays from childhood. He had also worked with and for the Richardsons of South London. He was a consummate liar whose inventiveness could well have earned him a fortune as a novelist had he had any talent for writing, and this is the major reason for treating his claims to know the truth about Mills's death with suspicion.

Johnny Bradbury was arrested in South Africa on a charge of murder. He was tried, found guilty and sentenced to death. At his trial, Bradbury told the jury that he'd been sent by a notorious London gang to frighten – definitely not to kill – Thomas 'Farmer' Waldeck, a con-man. Waldeck, who called himself a mineral prospector, had told his potential gulls that he had found perlite on a claim in the Transvaal. As might have been expected, the perlite mine was a myth, and those who'd been rubbing together their palms at the prospect of large and easy profits from an honest deal were extremely angry when they realized they had been double-crossed.

Johnny Bradbury and a hired South African thug repeatedly drove past

Waldeck's home, and when at last the con-man emerged on to his doorstep, Bradbury's companion fired. His aim was accurate, and Waldeck died. Bradbury was arrested.

It appeared probable that the East Ender would be executed for a crime which – according to him – he hadn't committed. Bradbury was a frightener, not a contract man. Seeing his only chance of escaping execution was to become of value to the police by implicating as many other villains as possible, he began to talk. His stories were so fascinating and adorned with such convincing detail that the South African police retailed them to Scotland Yard. Two British detectives flew out to interview Bradbury, and what he told them resulted in one of the largest clean-ups of London crime in history.

Whilst he was waiting to discover if his talking had saved his life, Bradbury was allowed to read the newspapers, where he learned of the arrival in South Africa of the son of the former heavyweight champion of the country. Bradbury also knew that in London the death of Mills had been headline news.

It is impossible to tell whether Bradbury had any knowledge at all about Mills's death or whether he invented his theories solely to increase his value – if alive – to British justice. At any rate, he now asked the prison governor to advise Donny that he had information about how and why Freddie had been murdered.

Donny McCorkindale wrote in detail to his mother and to Bill Bavin, Mills's old friend and property adviser, about his meeting with Johnny Bradbury in the cells of Pretoria Central Prison. Bradbury, as usual, had been only too ready to talk: the difficulty for Donny was in stopping him. Bradbury spoke with great gusto of his London activities and how he had advanced through the ranks of Richardson's South London gang until he had become its paymaster. He alleged that he had handed over £2,000 each week in bribes to West End Central police. The more he talked, the more fantastic became Bradbury's claims, and Donny began to fear that time would be up before Bradbury even broached the murder of Mills. So he bluntly interrupted and asked directly: 'Do you *really* know anything about my stepfather's murder? Was Freddie killed?'

Bradbury immediately and expansively admitted he had no firm evidence to support the story he was going to tell Donny, but emphasized that he had 'a very strong feeling about it'. He said the killer was the same man who had flown out to South Africa with him before Waldeck had been shot. He named the man concerned, gave details of his career, but could not provide any evidence to support his story.

On receiving her son's report, Chrissie Mills wrote to the Yard, laying her new – if extremely questionable – evidence before them, including the name of the villain finger-pointed by Bradbury. The police had no choice but to reopen their files on the death of Freddie Mills.

The detectives concentrated on interviewing everyone in the underworld who might be able to confirm or deny that Mills had been murdered. Inevitably they covered many of the same areas explored by their predecessors, and asked the same questions:

'Why had there been no suicide note?'

'How had the rifle reached the position in which Chrissie claimed to have found it?'

'What could have been the motive, if he had committed suicide?'

'Why had two shots been fired, one of which had passed through the front door of the car?'

'Why was there such a time-lag between Mills's arrival at the club and his being found dead?'

'Why had police reports about the position of the rifle changed?'

After three weeks of intensive investigation, Nipper Read came to the conclusion that Mrs Mills must have been mistaken about where the rifle had been when she got into the car beside her dead husband. He thought such an error hardly surprising seeing that Chrissie had been in a highly emotional state, having seen her white suit suddenly stained with her husband's blood.

Read was far more concerned with the absence of any suicide note than he was by the apparent absence of motive for suicide. A man as extrovert as Freddie Mills would be expected to leave some explanation for his actions if only to excuse himself for the dreadful blow he was inflicting on his wife and daughters. Men and women have been known to commit suicide on the spur of the moment, but they weren't usually of Mills's temperament. Nevertheless, the dividing line between sanity and madness can be frail.

The police, however, were still baffled by the absence of motive. To this day no one has propounded a really satisfying theory as to why this most popular of sportsmen should have taken his own life when he had so many reasons for wanting to live.

Read asked one new question: 'Why did Mills shoot himself through the eye?'

Eyes have a very special quality. They have been called 'the windows of the soul'. Many would-be suicides have been able to steel their nerves enough to put the muzzles of rifles to their foreheads or into their mouths, and pull the triggers. Few have chosen to fire through their eye and destroy their sight at the moment of death – so few, in fact, that the police have accepted this as a psychological factor, and suspect murder in such cases.

Eventually Read found a solution which satisfied him. If Mills had been holding the rifle lightly, with the muzzle pointing at the centre of his forehead, the kick of the gun – though very slight – could have snatched aside the point of the muzzle by the two or three inches necessary to send the bullet into the eye instead. It was a conceivable solution, if a doubtful one.

After the most careful investigation of the rumour that the Krays had been involved, Read decided that, for once, the twins had been defamed. There was nothing to connect them with the death. With the Krays locked up safely in prison cells, all their former associates and enemies were prepared – even eager – to tell the police everything and anything which might save themselves from prosecution. Having heard Chrissie Mills's account of her South African information, the police again interviewed all those whose evidence had helped convict the Krays. They asked every one of them: 'Have you heard anything to suggest that they murdered Freddie Mills?'

Despite the rumours, which had never abated, not a single person answered 'Yes.' Many of them added that had it been true, they would have known about it.

Charlie Richardson, who became a friend of his former rival when they were together in prison in the Isle of Wight, says that had Reggie been responsible for Mills's death he would have been quite incapable of keeping the matter to himself.

There is, however, another sound reason for arguing that the Krays had nothing to do with Mills's death. The twins had boxed as amateurs as well as professionals. Indeed, in the Thomas à Becket public house in the Old Kent Road, a famous boxing establishment, there is a poster on the wall opposite the bar with the names of Reggie and Ronnie Kray in supporting bouts at a tournament headed by Billy Ambrose, a very popular East End area champion. (Ambrose, who was also to fall foul of the law a few years later, made headlines when he escaped from the Scrubs in his pyjamas.)

The Krays' reputation as top-class boxers was extremely important to them. They were proud of their association with the boxing world and seldom missed a major tournament – indeed, they ran tournaments for charity. Among their closest friends were many leading fighters, and they employed ex-professional boxers in The Firm, always being prepared to give a hand-out to any old pug down on his luck. In pride of place on their mantelpieces were signed photographs of themselves with famous ring and theatre personalities: one of Ronnie sitting with Ted Kid Lewis and Sophie Tucker, the original Red Hot Mamma; another of Ronnie with Sonny Liston; and several of the twins and Freddie Mills.

The Krays respected, admired and liked boxers. The one virtue they esteemed above all others was courage, a virtue they possessed themselves. They understood better than most that every man who climbs through the ropes to fight has guts, and Freddie Mills was an outstandingly brave fighter. They would never have harmed him unless they were convinced he posed a real danger to their empire, and there is no evidence that Mills challenged them in any way. Not only would the Krays have been unlikely to harm Mills physically, they would have hesitated before demanding protection-money for his club.

It is too easy to assume that, because the Krays' web of crime was widespread, all night-clubs were paying them protection-money. It is not true. The Krays might be roughnecks – even in their Savile Row suits – but their organization was sophisticated. Their collectors were trained in Cable Street and Commercial Road but had to prove they could show judgement before they were posted 'up West'. The Krays used violence as a weapon, but Reggie was no fool. Whilst Ronnie might erupt physically at any moment, Reggie knew that unnecessary violence could easily lead to trouble. Occasionally a club behind with its weekly payments might be given a warning. Generally the proprietors would be given time to pay. If they genuinely couldn't find the money, there was little point in breaking up the premises or putting them out of business. It would have been counter-productive.

Mills wasn't the type of man to pay protection-money anyway. If any thug had tried to break up the Freddie Mills Nite Spot he would have ended in hospital. It is extremely unlikely that the Krays would ever have squeezed a man for whom they had such respect. If the club were handing out baksheesh, it was more likely to have been in the form of sweeteners to the police than ransom to the villains.

The police also concentrated again on trying to solve the mystery of those missing hours on Mills's last night. The press suggested that Mills had been drinking, after leaving Denmark Hill, at some unidentified flat r club. Yet no one came forward to say he or she had seen Mills that evening before his body was found in his car. Eventually, after questioning the club staff and Chrissie Mills again, the police accepted the evidence of Robert Deacon. He was a good witness; he had no apparent reason for distorting the truth. The police decided there were no missing hours.

According to Deacon, Mills had spoken of sleeping off the effects of a few drinks; yet at the inquest the pathologist had stated that the stomach had contained very little alcohol. How could they reconcile this apparent contradiction?

Mills was an athlete. Even though retired from the ring, he still trained daily and kept fit. He was certainly in far better physical condition than the normal man of his age. When a man is finely trained, he is far more susceptible to alcohol than he would be usually. Two tots of whisky or gin can have the same effect as half a bottle would on other people. If Mills had arrived at the club, as reported, and been told that it was almost empty, he might well have drowned his sorrows with a quick couple of brandies. The effect might have been almost immediate, and he might then have gone out to his car to 'sleep it off'. It is not a very satisfactory theory – too many 'mights'.

Once again the police closed their files, but Nipper Read still wasn't satisfied. He had failed to discover a satisfactory motive for Mills's taking his own life, and couldn't explain to his own satisfaction why there was no suicide note, or why there had been a second shot. And – to him of paramount importance – he couldn't really understand why Mills had shot into his eye.

Chrissie Mills was unswerving in her belief that her husband had been murdered, despite all the setbacks. This belief became obsessive, and immediately after the inquest she became deaf. No treatment had any effect. Doctors diagnosed that her deafness was brought about by shock. She remained in a world of semi-silence for more than seven years until she was cured by 'the laying on of hands'.

Again it appeared the full stop had been put to The Freddie Mills Story. It was not to be.

In November 1970, Mr Michael O'Halloran MP, the Labour Member of Parliament for Islington North, went to the police. A woman constituent whom he'd helped with her housing problems told him that Freddie Mills had been murdered. Her husband was in prison and he had heard gaol talk. He'd told her the name of the murderer.

Mr O'Halloran questioned her closely, and what she told him was so convincing that he said to the press: 'It was clearly my duty to go to the police.'

Scotland Yard, approached by reporters, confirmed that Mr O'Halloran had given them the name of the man, who – his constituent had said – had murdered Freddie Mills. They said he had given his information direct to the Yard. This was incorrect: had he done so, no doubt it would have been passed to Commander Virgo who had been in charge of the investigation five years earlier. Instead the Islington MP had informed a uniformed officer of his local force, which passed the information on to the Yard. But it never reached Virgo.

When Chrissie Mills was told of this new development, she said: 'I think people were paid to keep quiet and that's why the inquest didn't hear the truth.'

The police investigated this latest allegation but, after satisfying themselves there was little substance in the story, decided the files should remain closed. The young man cited by the constituent declared that any suggestion that he had had a hand in the murder of Freddie Mills was ridiculous. He blamed the story on a lover's tiff. 'What happened was my girl friend and I had a quarrel. It was only after that those stupid suggestions got about. I blame her.'

So another rumour had taken to the air. In the shadier environs of London, men whispered that all along they had known the truth . . . Freddie Mills was murdered. Of course, none of them dared to name the killer.

# 16

THE most persistent of all the rumours was that the Krays had had Mills murdered. Despite there being not the slightest evidence to support this theory, it recurred again and again. Perhaps its endurance stemmed from the fact that after their imprisonment the Krays became the popular scapegoats for all unsolved crime . . . after all, there was no one left to defend them. Shady characters who did not like to admit that they had no inside information found it easy to whisper out of the corner of their mouths: 'Of course, don't tell anyone I told you, but The Firm hadn't liked . . .'

Charlie Kray, the elder brother of the infamous twins, was sentenced to ten years for his share in The Firm's criminal activities. Today, having served his sentence, he claims his imprisonment was a gross injustice and that he had kept his hands clean throughout his brothers' reign. Be that as it may, today the white-haired, well-groomed and affable Charlie Kray would pass anywhere as a successful businessman, maybe with theatrical connections. He talks confidently and says he has put all the past behind him; he is building his future as 'Charlie Kray' and not as the brother of the notorious twins.

His present mood of independence is essential as he is not at the moment over-popular with his brothers. This certainly is not his fault. The film based on the Krays' lives raked in far more money than any of them had anticipated. Since Reggie was in prison and Ronnie in Broadmoor, the negotiations were left to Charlie. In today's rather grey environment, the gangster wars of twenty-five to thirty years ago aroused tremendous interest at the box office. No one could have known this in advance, but the brothers have been critical of Charlie for not making a better financial deal on their behalf.

From inside prison, Reggie Kray has fathered a successful commercial company which is managed by young men he met while they were serving sentences. The company is largely concerned with charitable ventures. It has been widely suggested that Reggie hopes these virtuous activities will impress the parole board favourably and might bring about a reduction in his sentence.

There can be no such hopes for Ronnie in the asylum for the criminally insane. His future rests more with psychiatrists than a parole board. Despite his acknowledged homosexuality, he has married and his bride was no publicity-seeking starlet; no bimbo wanting fleeting notoriety or limelight. She is a mature, smart and attractive woman who has built up a most successful business.

Despite the present lack of warmth between the twins and their brother, Charlie is quick to defend them against any accusations he believes are unjust, since over the years many unsolved crimes have been laid at their door.

Lunching with Charlie Kray, I asked him directly about the suggestion that his brothers had either killed Freddie Mills or had given the orders for him to be shot. He thought the idea totally ridiculous: 'How could my brothers, who loved boxing and boxers, have harmed a man who had fought his way to a world championship and who had been one of their friends?'

I pointed out that friendship had not prevented their murdering one of their former associates, Jack the Hat.

Charlie Kray said that was an entirely different case. Mills was one of their heroes. When they'd heard that the Mills Nite Spot was doing badly, they had made a point of sending their friends there. He thought the question of protection-money was equally ridiculous. 'Why should anyone demand protection-money from an establishment which was plainly going to the wall?'

I also asked Charlie Kray whether jealousy might have been a motive for Ronnie wanting Mills eliminated, and mentioned ballad-singer Michael Holliday. Charlie dismissed this as not worth consideration. He was adamant that as far as he knew Ronnie had never even met the singer.

If there is not the remotest evidence that the Krays had any connection with Mills's death, another fantasy is that the Richardson brothers were responsible. This legend differs from that of the Krays in that it didn't emerge in the cafés of Soho until the publication of Bill Bavin's book *The Strange Death of Freddie Mills*. Whereas there is again no evidence to sustain this accusation, Bill Bavin provided enough details to encourage speculation.

Bavin is one of many men claiming a close friendship with the dead man. I met him when he was researching for *The Strange Death of Freddie Mills*, and though we were in total agreement that Mills did not commit suicide, the suggestion in his book that the Richardsons were responsible amazed me because I couldn't see that he had a trace of evidence to support his suggestion – other than the wild assertions made by the criminal, Johnny Bradbury, who'd been associated with the Richardsons. Bavin interviewed Bradbury when the criminal was serving his life sentence in South Africa for murder.

It is my opinion that Bavin's suggestion that the Richardsons had had a hand in Mills's death is without foundation. However, the reader should know that my opinion could be biased: I am a close personal friend of Charlie Richardson, the elder brother and leader of the gang, who became notorious when stories of vicious torture made the headlines.

Charlie was sentenced in Number One Court at the Old Bailey to twenty-five years' imprisonment; only five years fewer than Reggie and Ronnie Kray.

Perhaps the reason for the savageness of his sentence was the abhorrence of the judge, jury and public at the tale, given in evidence, about how he had 'nailed one of his enemies to the floor through the foot'. Charlie swore to me that this was a myth. I didn't believe him. However, three years later I was chatting in the Belsize Arms with Professor Lippman Kessel MBE (Mil) MC FRCS, orthopaedic consultant at the Royal Orthopaedic Hospital. The professor had no knowledge of my relationship with Charlie Richardson when he started inveighing against British law and saying how much he preferred the French system of examining magistrate seeking the truth, rather than our adversarial trial. He told how he had been asked to examine the foot of a man who, it was alleged, had been nailed to the floor by a villain called 'Richardson'. The professor had declared the story a myth, since the wound was at least six years old though it was said by the prosecution to have been inflicted only the previous year. However, this fact had been glossed over by the prosecution as it didn't further their case.

In prison Charlie, who has a fine brain, studied psychology, and claims today that his whole appreciation of the value of life was changed dramatically by reading *Battle for the Mind* by the late Dr William Sargant, perhaps the most controversial psychiatrist to practise in this century and, coincidentally, also a close friend of mine for more than twenty-five years.

Having served fourteen years of his sentence Charlie decided to escape. He had three reasons for deciding to go 'on the run'. Firstly, he had observed that after serving fourteen years many convicts suffered sudden and irreversible mental deterioration. He told me: 'One day a man would be talking to you sensibly and the next day there'd be nothing behind the windows of his eyes.'

Secondly, he believed that our parole system was a form of torture as vicious mentally as any of the physical crimes of which he'd been accused. The applicant for parole needed to behave impeccably as he waited for his hearing, ticking off each passing day on his calendar. After his parole interview he would be told nothing. Later he would receive a typed note informing him that his application had been rejected. No reasons and no explanations would be given. He would then have to continue to live a lickspittle existence, once again, as he began ticking off the days until his next application was allowed.

Thirdly, he considered his sentence had been excessive. He told me: 'Tony, I never endangered a member of the public. It was warfare between gangs, villain against villain. I never killed or murdered anyone. Today if a man goes into a post office with a gun and shoots the postmistress he will serve twelve years at the most. I'm serving twenty-five years for far less serious crimes. I deserved ten years at the most.'

Charlie was a product of his time and suffered because of it. In the 1960s, with the public daily becoming aware of the almost open gang-warfare and reading in the press that the American Mafia was on the point of taking over British gambling, the judiciary began to hand out sentences far longer than had been known up to that time. I did not disapprove of this trend towards longer sentences, but I believed that if we were to put men behind bars for the major part of their adult lives we had to treat them humanely. I believe the British retain a Victorian taste for punishment for its own sake, and no one seems to find it obscene that we are shutting men up for fifteen, twenty or thirty years in almost medieval conditions – two or even three prisoners confined for twenty-three out of every twenty-four hours in a cell designed to lodge a single man. There are no lavatories in the cells so that every morning the convict is degraded by the loathsome tradition of 'slopping out'. And there is no work or training to occupy the mind or prepare the man for his return to society.

I was also deeply worried by the effects these long sentences would have on the wives and families of the criminals. How could a woman be expected to remain faithful for almost the whole of her sexually active life when she was only occasionally allowed to touch her man openly across a table, with a warder listening and surrounded by other prisoners and their families? In more enlightened countries 'conjugal visits' are arranged to try and solve the problem of sexual separation. How can children be brought up to love and respect a father who is almost a total stranger to them?

I persuaded BBC Radio 4 to let me write an investigative documentary on the subject for inclusion in the 'Radio 4 Reports' series. In the course of my research, I discovered that the wives of several long-serving prisoners had got together for mutual support and to campaign for a reduction of their men's sentences. The organizer was Maureen Richardson, the wife of Charlie's younger brother Eddie, who was serving fifteen years. Maureen became the linchpin of my programme. She was most appreciative that I avoided naming her two daughters, and kept them out of the programme, lest the publicity hurt them at school. After all, being known as the daughters of an infamous torturer would hardly be an ideal launching-pad for their careers.

A few years later I met Maureen again. For one of my programmes in my series 'Lifelines of Medicine' I went to interview Annette Spence, the Advice Sister at the Family Planning Association in Mortimer Street. Maureen had taken a job as receptionist there. Over the years she'd been hurt so often by people's thoughtlessness that she assumed I'd tell her employers her identity. Of course, I did nothing of the sort.

As a result, when her brother-in-law escaped from prison to make his three objections to our penal system and they wanted a journalist they could trust to present his views, Maureen put forward my name. Maureen and Eddie – who by then had served his sentence – invited me to dinner in their comfortable country home. Would I meet Charlie and discuss the position with him? As a journalist I agreed on the spot to present his arguments. Eventually I set out his views on the front page of the *Sunday Times*, but before committing myself to the best way to break the story, I turned to my long-time employers – although I was freelance – BBC Radio. The Head of the Talks and Documentary section was ecstatic at the prospect of being first with such a dramatic story. Few such chances came the way of old-fashioned 'steam radio'. They issued me with a UHER recorder and a parcel of tapes.

Unfortunately by the time I had recorded Charlie and returned to Broadcasting House – delighted with the results for Charlie had spoken eloquently – the Corporation lawyers had intervened, and the police had been alerted.

In the presence of my solicitor – on my insistence – I was interviewed by a Chief Superintendent. He agreed that as I had offered Charlie no financial support, and as I did not know his address, I had committed no criminal offence. He told me I should get in touch with them the moment I knew where he was so they could arrest him. To this instruction I answered with a terse: 'Not bloody likely!' The Chief Superintendent wasn't surprised and said with a smile that in my position he'd probably give a similar response.

The press was quick to criticize the BBC for handing over one of their long-time reporters to the police – criticism that did me no favour because it killed my popularity with that particular department. It might, of course, have been only coincidental that my long-running series 'Lifelines of Medicine' came to an end shortly afterwards. The Richardson story cost me dearly.

Today the Richardson brothers have gone their separate ways. Eddie, despite having a successful metal business and a luxurious home, has been unable to resist the lure of big money, and in 1990 he was sentenced to thirty years' imprisonment for drug offences involving more than £78 million. Charlie, very much the more intellectual of the two, has established himself as a businessman, concentrating on mining in Uganda. He has never tried to conceal his identity or past history from any of the industrialists with whom he has had dealings, and without doubt his openness has earned him considerable respect, though the publicity surrounding his brother's case has proved an embarrassment. The villainy of his former life has been put behind him. He is small but muscular, bearded, dapper, favouring Savile Row suits and with a quiet sense of humour, and it is difficult today to detect any trace of the gangster who was second only to Ronnie Kray in notoriety.

Naturally I have discussed Bill Bavin's suggestions at length with Charlie Richardson, to whom I gave a copy of *The Strange Death of Freddie Mills*. Charlie was contemptuous of the talk that 'protection-money' had been paid by clubs. He has told me – and his opinion is supported by Nipper Read's statements about police being in the Krays' pay – that a large percentage of the police covering the West End were 'on the take'. Most of the officers accepted that they could go into night-clubs such as the Freddie Mills Nite Spot and entertain their friends without being presented with the bill. Why, therefore, should club owners pay outside gangs for protection when they had friends on the Force to safeguard their interests?

Like the Kray twins, both Charlie and Eddie Richardson had been first-class boxers and the argument against the Krays' harming a leading fighter – one of their 'fraternity' – also applied to the Richardsons.

Another reason to doubt the involvement of the Richardsons was that their activities were concentrated south of the river. It was only later, when Charlie was mining in South Africa, that Eddie, without his brother's shrewd advice, moved up West. His foolhardiness resulted in an inter-gang shoot-out during which Eddie was wounded in the bottom. This fracas led to the Richardsons' downfall and eventually to their lengthy prison sentences.

In *Rough Justice*, Robert Parker writes at length about the Waldeck murder and John Bradbury's wild allegations. Charlie Richardson has never denied that some of his activities in South Africa wouldn't have borne close examination, but he finds the suggestion that he would have employed the loose-tongued John Bradbury as a hit-man totally ridiculous.

'Bradbury', he says, 'was a notorious liar who couldn't tell the difference between truth and fantasy. He was always a small-time thief on the fringe of London crime. He told the police what they wanted to hear in the hope of earning himself remission.'

There is not the slightest evidence to tie the Richardsons to Mills's death. They had no motive and, as keen sportsmen, would have been more likely to dig deep in their pockets to help Mills had they known he was in financial trouble, than to harm him. Charlie Richardson is of the opinion that Mills committed suicide, being one of the many ex-criminals who still believe Mills was about to be arrested for the murders of the Hammersmith prostitutes.

He was, not surprisingly, extremely angry at Bill Bavin's suggestion that he and his brother Eddie had been involved in any way. 'Why', he asks, 'did Bavin go to such pains to prove Mills was a victim of a London gang?'

He had his own answer to this question: 'Bavin must for some reason have a guilty conscience about the death of his friend, the ex-world champion.' He points out that Bavin handled all Freddie's property deals, buying several houses and a row of terrace homes on Mills's behalf. Yet at his death Mills left only a pittance. Had Bavin himself something to hide? Was he pointing a finger at everyone else, Richardson wondered, to divert attention from his own activities on Mills's behalf?

It is a fair question. In 1957, according to the author, Mills was earning more than £3,000 a year from the property he had bought on the advice of Bill Bavin. Later, the boxer appointed another manager and the properties were generally allowed to deteriorate. Nevertheless, at the market value of the time Mills's properties must have been worth, at the very least, £20,000 – a sum that does not include the value of his club premises, which was in excess of £6,000. Nor did it include the value of Joggi Villa, on which Mills owed £4,000.

Yet after Mills's death, as we have seen, no one could discover what Mills had done with that money. To this day it remains a mystery.

# 17

DURING his career Mills took far too many punches to his head for his own good. Even the most fervent boxing supporters agree that boxing is a dangerous occupation; however, it is also true that it teaches discipline and builds self-confidence. But it would be irresponsible to examine the life and death of Freddie Mills without asking whether the punishment he took in the ring caused, or contributed to, his death.

Among the legion of rumours as to why he might have committed suicide, the suggestion that he could have killed himself because he realized his mind was deteriorating – that he was becoming punch-drunk – has seldom been mentioned. Boxing people prefer to brush this subject under the carpet. Neurologists, however, claim that it is impossible for a boxer to be punched about the head as frequently as was Mills without there being any after-effects.

Was Mills punch-drunk? Could he have detected the early symptoms of this condition in himself and, as a fiercely proud man, been unable to face the mental deterioration which would have been his lot?

Many more sociologically and medically enlightened countries have already banned boxing, while in others amateur boxing is permitted though professional boxing is outlawed. The argument for this is that a modern, civilized society should not pay young men to risk scrambling their brains for the sake of entertainment.

It is not surprising that many self-dubbed 'sportsmen' vigorously oppose this principle – none more so than those with financial interests in the industry. They contend that there is no such condition as punch-drunkenness; or that if there is, it is a thing of the past. They claim that the sport today is so rigidly and well controlled, and the medical examinations before contests are so thorough, that boxers' brains are safe from damage. Sadly, this reasoning doesn't stand up to analytical examination. Like mining, boxing by its nature can never be *safe*, even though all the safety precautions are valuable. Working underground will always be perilous: being punched on the head will always involve danger to the brain. As I have already said, boxing is the only legal activity, let alone sport, in which the aim is to render someone unconscious.

The skull, which contains the brain, is not a smooth, hollow globe, but has bony reefs as well as stiff and sharp parchment-like strips of membrane. The brain itself is of a thick, table-jelly consistency. If you handle a fresh human brain you will find it so vulnerable that your fingers can only too easily break through the tissue. The 'grey matter' – the most vital part of the brain – lies directly beneath the dura – the containing membrane – and so is particularly easily damaged.

When a punch lands – especially a hook or a swing rather than a straight blow – the whole head twists. The container – the skull – slews around before coming to a jolting stop as it reaches the limit of its movement. The brain, not attached to the skull but free to move loosely, accelerates to catch up with its bone container and, unavoidably, is dashed against the reefs and sharp membranes. Any resultant tearing will cause irreparable damage.

Punches can have immediate or delayed effect. Whilst a single punch may cause an instantaneous cerebral haemorrhage, recurrent punches, taken over a long period, can cause damage even though the symptoms may not appear for many years.

The pro-boxing lobby argues that if blows to the head caused brain damage, many footballers would be affected by heading the ball. This ignores the difference between receiving a punch and heading a football. The footballer makes a conscious decision to head the ball: he tenses his neck muscles in preparation, and the impact of the ball does not twist the head. The punch only lands because the boxer does *not* anticipate it. He is not prepared, and so the head is thrust sideways.

There have been several comprehensive medical reports on punch-drunkenness or, to give the condition its medical term, post-traumatic encephalopathy. The expression 'punch-drunk' is a perfectly accurate description of its symptoms. The afflicted boxer has impaired memory, his speech becomes lisping and incoherent. His reflexes slow, and his gait turns into the stagger and shuffle of a drunken man. He will suffer personality changes, so that the once gentle and self-controlled gentleman can suddenly commit acts of violence.

When the British Medical Association first called for the abolition of boxing, the resolution passed by the committee was more emotional than logical, and the British Boxing Board of Control had acceptable reasons for refusing to co-operate because they had not been given the opportunity of arguing their case or laying their wide experience before the doctors. However, since then there have been several international medical investigations and every one has stated categorically that punches to the head cause brain damage.

Dr Helen Grant, former neuropathologist of the Charing Cross Hospital, has even been able to demonstrate clearly which area of the brain has been damaged by punching. When Cassius Clay, aka Muhammad Ali, who rightly dubbed himself 'the Greatest', degenerated into an incoherent wreck within ten years of hanging up his gloves, boxing defenders claimed that he wasn't punch-drunk but was suffering from Parkinson's Disease. Today it can be shown that the part of the brain affected by punches corresponds with the areas attacked by other neurological conditions like Parkinson's. If Muhammad Ali has Parkinson's, it is a convenient coincidence.

In 1973, a group of doctors led by Professor J.A.N. Corsellis, a neuropathologist, published a report, *The Aftermath of Boxing*. This report was based on the study of men who had been boxing between 1900 and 1940, half of whom had either had more than 300 contests or had been boxing for more than fifteen years. Of these, more than 50 per cent had suffered brain damage. In 1987, Professor Corsellis issued another report compiled during his retirement, which substantiated his earlier findings.

Since 1973 far more evidence as to the damage caused by a punch or by punches to the head has been gathered. In 1984, the BMA set up a committee to study the subject: their report stated:

Brain scanning techniques now enable brain damage to be detected during life. The abnormalities found correspond closely to those previously reported from post-mortem studies. Brain damage previously associated with the punch-drunk syndrome is now being detected before obvious clinical signs have developed. In the past these lesions were undetected because of the limitations of traditional tests. Brain scan evidence of cerebral atrophy has now been found in comparatively young boxers, including amateurs and those whose careers have been considered successful.

The report concluded: 'The Board of Science and Education regrets that the British Boxing Board of Control appeared unwilling to co-operate with its working party.'

The BBBC points out, justifiably, that boxing is safer today than it has ever been. Board rules ensure that boxers are examined medically before they are allowed into the ring, and two doctors are in attendance at every licensed tournament. However, they are not empowered to stop a fight when they consider a boxer at risk. This decision is left to the referee. The argument in favour of this system is that only the referee is close enough to look into a boxer's eyes. Oddly, however, referees do not have any medical training.

There is no medical examination before sparring during training. This is important because often when a champion is preparing for a big contest, he has to go all out against his sparring-partners; he can't afford to pull punches. A sparring-partner often has to take quite unacceptable punishment without a doctor being present to call a halt when he is in danger of being badly hurt.

In some countries the wearing of headguards is compulsory. These do protect eyebrows from cuts but they do nothing to protect the brain, for hooks and swings can still jerk the head violently. This form of safeguard has rightly been rejected by the BBBC.

The pro-boxing fraternity often challenges its critics to name any modern-day boxer who is punch-drunk. This is a safe gambit: any boxer described publicly as being punch-drunk has a sound legal case against the citizen naming him, since he could claim that any prospective employer would be unlikely to hire a man whose behaviour is unpredictable. However, no one who has spent any years actively in the boxing industry can swear on oath that he has never seen the shambling old men who haunt dressing-rooms in the hope of cadging a few pence from the up-and-coming youngsters.

The boxing lobby argues that if boxing were made illegal, unlicensed tournaments would flourish. This is true. But running unlicensed shows would lay all those taking part – promoters, match-makers, managers, referees, seconds, trainers and boxers – open to prosecution. Dog fights are still staged illicitly but are not nearly as commonplace as they would be were they permitted by law. But even the tournaments run today under the auspices of the BBBC are of dubious legality, though the position is by no means clear-cut and prosecution is rare. After all, every boxer commits GBH – grievous bodily harm – on his opponent if he can. He is only protected by the legal umbrella of the BBBC, which is a self-elected and self-perpetuating body.

Those with a financial interest in boxing frequently refer to the number of boxers who have taken part in dozens of contests, have taken hundreds of hard punches, and yet show no symptoms of mental damage. Again this is true. But no two humans are identical. If the brain fits snugly into the skull, it will move more in kilter with its bony container than if it is loose, and the damage will be minimal. On the other hand if the brain is loose in the skull it will be dashed against it when the head rotates after a blow. So it isn't surprising that while one boxer remains apparently undamaged another will end up his days in a mental ward. To say that punch-drunkenness does not exist because some boxers show no signs of brain damage is as illogical as the plea of the tobacco manufacturers that smoking doesn't damage the health because some smokers live into old age.

I have known many punch-drunk boxers. Some of them, in the early days of mental deterioration, can mask their symptoms by leading the conversation on to subjects for which they have rehearsed speeches. Investigators into post-traumatic encephalopathy have observed the repetitive use of expressions and anecdotes, an intelligent use of the boxer's remaining mental capacities which may very likely enable him to hide the mental damage he has sustained for a considerable period . . . at least from those with no particular interest in the subject. Yet invariably with age, as the blood supply to the brain becomes less efficient, unconcealable symptoms will present themselves. For many years after he retired, the great flyweight, Jimmy Wilde – the Ghost with a Hammer in his Hand – was pointed to by Welsh fight-fans as an example of a boxer who had had hundreds of contests and suffered no mental harm. Sadly, the years caught up with him, and when I wrote his story as a radio play for the BBC his memory had gone. That alone might not have mattered terribly, but he was also no longer responsible for his behaviour. He ended his days as a patient in a mental ward.

Because of his aggressive style, Freddie Mills took many vicious blows to his head. Because he was often matched with much taller and heavier men, he was bound to take more blows to the head than to the body. His opponents would have to punch downwards to be on the target as Mills crouched and weaved his way to get within close range. It would be most surprising if he had suffered no ill-effects in a career which took him from the seaside booth to the Royal Albert Hall.

Nevertheless, after his retirement, Mills derived considerable pleasure from defending his sport at every opportunity. He delighted in describing how a visiting American neurologist, having put him through a series of tests, said that he not only showed no signs of mental deterioration but had a higher than average IQ. In the public debate against Dr Edith Summerskill MP already described, he acted as second to Jack Solomons. But at the height of the argument, Dr Summerskill drew attention to Mills's sudden loss of words. This, she claimed, was 'very revealing'.

Neither his high IQ nor his ability to perform on stage, TV or radio can rule out the probability that he had suffered brain damage to some extent. Mills's *amour propre* was of the utmost importance to him; if he had even suspected that his memory was beginning to play him up or his reflexes were slowing, he might well have felt unable to face the future. In those early-morning hours when molehills can inflate in the imagination until they become Everests, he might well have pictured himself as a target for amusement or contempt. If his public began to laugh at him instead of with him, he might well have decided, life held nothing more worth while.

# EPILOGUE

NATURALLY, having been the inspector for many of his contests and having worked in cabaret with him after his retirement, I have been intensely interested in the rumours and theories surrounding Freddie Mills's death. Since I first asked on radio, 'Was it suicide or murder?' I have changed my opinion on certain points.

Initially I had agreed with Jack Solomons, Teddy Waltham and many others from the boxing world that Mills wasn't a 'suicide type'. But in my series 'Lifelines of Medicine', and whilst researching for a programme and book on depression, I talked about suicide with several leading psychiatrists including Dr William Sargant, my close friend; Dr Desmond Kelly of Roehampton; and Dr Anthony Storr of Oxford who has written on human violence. Through them I have become aware of the intricacies of the mind and the unpredictability of those suffering from certain mental conditions. Now I realize that when a person decides to take his or her own life, he or she is invariably unbalanced, and that no one can confidently predict such a person's reaction to a set of circumstances. The most an experienced psychiatrist can say is: 'Under these conditions he or she *might* do so and so.' The old verdict 'suicide while the balance of mind was disturbed' was a good description in most cases.

The only motive which seems to me to hold water – though it is never mentioned in boxing circles – would be that Freddie feared he was becoming punch-drunk. Again and again in later years he referred to his first contest against Gus Lesnevich: 'After that sort of bashing a man cannot be the same again. The brain must be affected.' If Freddie Mills had detected a thickening in his speech, a loss of memory or a lack of co-ordination in his movements, he might have suspected that he was suffering the first symptoms of punch-drunkenness. If so, he might have found it impossible to contemplate himself becoming a stumbling wreck.

However, though I now believe that despite his outgoing character

Mills *could* have taken his own life, I am convinced that in fact he did not do so, but was murdered.

The facts that weigh most heavily with me against his having committed suicide are his courage, and the fact that the shot was put through his eye. My doubts are reinforced by the position of the gun as Chrissie Mills found it, and the trial shot through the passenger door. Neither of these is, to my mind, explicable if Mills shot himself. And how, if he were planning to kill himself, could he have played and joked with his children, and fooled around with friends, without revealing his feelings?

The aspect of the case which most surprised me during my researches is how perfunctory much of the original inquiry was. The evidence given at the inquest was contradictory in many significant respects. Certainly the police's own version of events, such as the position of the gun, was inconsistent. But what seemed to me to be obvious lines of inquiry were never pursued: the discrepancies in time were not exposed, nor was the failure of the doorman and head-waiter to have mentioned the blood cascading down the right-hand side of Mills's face when they tried to waken him.

One can only consider that the coroner's verdict was, from the police point of view, an extremely convenient one. They were already heavily involved with the most complex investigations into gang warfare in London and the possibility of a Mafia invasion. Further inquiries into this case might well have resulted in their having to expose more about their own operations than they would have wished. A verdict of suicide might well have been one they were ready to accept, in spite of the questions it left unanswered. And by the time Nipper Read reopened the case, years had passed and the trail was cold.

If Mills, then, didn't pull the trigger, who did?

As I have shown, there is no sound evidence against either the Krays or the Richardsons. The Krays had become convenient scapegoats who could safely be blamed for any unsolved crime, while the only accusation against the Richardsons was that of a murderer who was pointing the finger at anyone in his anxiousness to please his gaolers.

But there was one other rumour which came to my ears fairly late in my inquiries, when I spent a couple of days filming in Smithfield Market for my 1989 TV documentary on punch-drunkenness, *The Purse*. There I heard for the first time the suggestion that a Chinese tong had been responsible for Mills's death. Big Den, one of the real characters of the Market and a man who had been feeding me dud greyhound tips for years, told me: 'Mills was killed by a Chinese gang who wanted to take over his club. Everyone in the Market knows that.'

I hadn't known. But as I researched further, I found that a substantial body of opinion held that the Chinese, who had no great respect for British sporting figures, had watched Mills's growing involvement with the Chinese community in Soho with interest. First he had owned a Chinese restaurant; now he was in partnership in the night-club with Andy Ho. A tong, part of whose business was opium-peddling, had needed a headquarters in Soho. The yard at the back of the Freddie Mills Nite Spot was in the shadows; dope merchants could have come and gone safely without being seen by the patrolling vice-squad. Mills, it was said, had rejected the tong's repeated approaches, and had forfeited his life as a result.

My attempts to investigate the truth of this have been inconclusive. I did manage to reach two Chinese who, according to my informant, had been gangsters at the time. They wouldn't talk. A friend with a long prison record pointed the finger at a Chinese businessman who frequented a Chinese restaurant in W2. Before I could talk to him the police had beaten me to it and he is now serving a long sentence and 'unavailable for comment'.

If a Chinese gang, wanting to take over the club of which Mills was so proud, did execute him, many of the mysteries would be solved. This seems to me to be the likeliest solution.

If he was not the victim of a gang killing, then he must have been shot by an individual enemy who, after killing him, tried to make it look like suicide. There is no evidence as to who this personal enemy might have been, and it appeared to the world at large that the popular ex-champion had no enemies. There again, it seems more likely that Mr Mills the night-club owner was murdered, than Freddie Mills the great and brave fighter.

Chrissie Mills has never ceased to believe that her husband was murdered, and points as evidence to the sinister visitor who warned her off, alluding to 'people who are interested in the case'. On the other hand, Commander Read is equally sure Mills took his own life.

Will the truth one day be revealed? Or can the full-stop never be added to the Freddie Mills story?

# Discover more about our forthcoming books through Penguin's FREE newspaper...

**Penguin**
 Quarterly

## It's packed with:

- exciting features
- author interviews
- previews & reviews
- books from your favourite films & TV series
- exclusive competitions & much, much more...

**Write off for your free copy today to:**
Dept JC
Penguin Books Ltd
FREEPOST
West Drayton
Middlesex
UB7 0BR
NO STAMP REQUIRED

# READ MORE IN PENGUIN

In every corner of the world, on every subject under the sun, Penguin represents quality and variety – the very best in publishing today.

For complete information about books available from Penguin – including Puffins, Penguin Classics and Arkana – and how to order them, write to us at the appropriate address below. Please note that for copyright reasons the selection of books varies from country to country.

**In the United Kingdom:** Please write to *Dept. JC, Penguin Books Ltd, FREEPOST, West Drayton, Middlesex UB7 OBR*

If you have any difficulty in obtaining a title, please send your order with the correct money, plus ten per cent for postage and packaging, to *PO Box No. 11, West Drayton, Middlesex UB7 OBR*

**In the United States:** Please write to *Penguin USA Inc., 375 Hudson Street, New York, NY 10014*

**In Canada:** Please write to *Penguin Books Canada Ltd, 10 Alcorn Avenue, Suite 300, Toronto, Ontario M4V 3B2*

**In Australia:** Please write to *Penguin Books Australia Ltd, 487 Maroondah Highway, Ringwood, Victoria 3134*

**In New Zealand:** Please write to *Penguin Books (NZ) Ltd,182–190 Wairau Road, Private Bag, Takapuna, Auckland 9*

**In India:** Please write to *Penguin Books India Pvt Ltd, 706 Eros Apartments, 56 Nehru Place, New Delhi 110 019*

**In the Netherlands:** Please write to *Penguin Books Netherlands B.V., Keizersgracht 231 NL–1016 DV Amsterdam*

**In Germany:** Please write to *Penguin Books Deutschland GmbH, Friedrichstrasse 10–12, W–6000 Frankfurt/Main 1*

**In Spain:** Please write to *Penguin Books S. A., C. San Bernardo 117–6° E–28015 Madrid*

**In Italy:** Please write to *Penguin Italia s.r.l., Via Felice Casati 20, I–20124 Milano*

**In France:** Please write to *Penguin France S. A., 17 rue Lejeune, F–31000 Toulouse*

**In Japan:** Please write to *Penguin Books Japan, Ishikiribashi Building, 2–5–4, Suido, Tokyo 112*

**In Greece:** Please write to *Penguin Hellas Ltd, Dimocritou 3, GR–106 71 Athens*

**In South Africa:** Please write to *Longman Penguin Southern Africa (Pty) Ltd, Private Bag X08, Bertsham 2013*

# READ MORE IN PENGUIN

## A CHOICE OF NON-FICTION

**Citizens** A Chronicle of the French Revolution   Simon Schama

'The most marvellous book I have read about the French Revolution in the last fifty years' – Richard Cobb in *The Times*. 'He has chronicled the vicissitudes of that world with matchless understanding, wisdom, pity and truth, in the pages of this huge and marvellous book' – *Sunday Times*

**Out of Africa**   Karen Blixen (Isak Dinesen)

Karen Blixen went to Kenya in 1914 to run a coffee-farm; its failure in 1931 caused her to return to Denmark where she wrote this classic account of her experiences. 'A work of sincere power ... a fine lyrical study of life in East Africa' – Harold Nicolson in the *Daily Telegraph*

**Yours Etc.**   Graham Greene
Letters to the Press 1945–1989

'An entertaining celebration of Graham Greene's lesser-known career as a prolific author of letters to newspapers; you will find unarguable proof of his total addiction to everything about his time, from the greatest issues of the day to the humblest subjects imaginable' – Salman Rushdie in the *Observer*

**The Trial of Lady Chatterley**   Edited By C. H. Rolph

In October 1960 at the Old Bailey a jury of nine men and three women prepared for the infamous trial of *Lady Chatterley's Lover*. The Obscene Publications Act had been introduced the previous year and D. H. Lawrence's notorious novel was the first to be prosecuted under its provisions. This is the account of the historic trial and acquittal of Penguin Books.

**Handbook for the Positive Revolution**   Edward de Bono

Edward de Bono's challenging new book provides a practical framework for a serious revolution which has no enemies but seeks to make things better. The hand symbolizes the five basic principles of the Positive Revolution, to remind us that even a small contribution is better than endless criticism.

# READ MORE IN PENGUIN

## A CHOICE OF NON-FICTION

**The Time Out Film Guide**   Edited by Tom Milne

The definitive, up-to-the minute directory of over 9,500 films – world cinema from classics and silent epics to reissues and the latest releases – assessed by two decades of *Time Out* reviewers. 'In my opinion the best and most comprehensive' – Barry Norman

**The Remarkable Expedition**   Olivia Manning

The events of an extraordinary attempt in 1887 to rescue Emin Pasha, Governor of Equatoria, are recounted here by the author of *The Balkan Trilogy* and *The Levant Trilogy* and vividly reveal unprecedented heights of magnificent folly in the perennial human search for glorious conquest.

**Berlin: Coming in From the Cold**   Ken Smith

'He covers everything from the fate of the ferocious-looking dogs that formerly helped to guard East Germany's borders to the vast Orwellian apparatus that maintained security in the now-defunct German Democratic Republic ... a pithy style and an eye for the telling detail' – *Independent*

**Cider with Rosie/As I Walked Out one Midsummer Morning**
Laurie Lee

Now together in one volume, Laurie Lee's two classic autobiographical works, *Cider with Rosie* and *As I Walked Out One Midsummer Morning*. Together they illustrate Laurie Lee's superb descriptive powers as he conveys the poignancy of a boy's transformation into adulthood.

**In the Land of Oz**   Howard Jacobson

'A wildly funny account of his travels; abounding in sharp characterization, crunching dialogue and self-parody, it actually is a book which makes you laugh out loud on almost every page ... sharp, skilful and brilliantly funny' – *Literary Review*

# READ MORE IN PENGUIN

## A CHOICE OF NON-FICTION

**Bernard Shaw**  Michael Holroyd
Volume 2 1898–1918 The Pursuit of Power

'A man whose art rested so much upon the exercise of intelligence could not have chosen a more intelligent biographer ... The pursuit of Bernard Shaw has grown, and turned into a pursuit of the whole twentieth century' – Peter Ackroyd in *The Times*

**Shots from the Hip**  Charles Shaar Murray

His classic encapsulation of the moment when rock stars turned junkies as the sixties died; his dissection of rock 'n' roll violence as citizens assaulted the Sex Pistols; superstar encounters from the decline of Paul McCartney to Mick Jagger's request that the author should leave – Charles Shaar Murray's *Shots From the Hip* is also rock history in the making.

**Managing on the Edge**  Richard Pascale

The co-author of the bestselling *The Art of Japanese Management* has once again turned conventional thinking upside down. Conflict and contention in organizations are not just unavoidable – they are positively to be welcomed. The successes and failures of large corporations can help us understand the need to maintain a creative tension between fitting companies together and splitting them apart.

**Just Looking**  John Updike

'Mr Updike can be a very good art critic, and some of these essays are marvellous  examples of critical explanation ... a deep understanding of the art emerges ... His reviews of some recent and widely attended shows ... quite surpass the modest disclaimer of the title' – *The New York Times Book Review*

**Shelley: The Pursuit**  Richard Holmes

'Surely the best biography of Shelley ever written ... He makes Shelley's character entirely convincing by showing us the poet at every stage of his development acting upon, and reacting to, people and events' – Stephen Spender

# READ MORE IN PENGUIN

## A CHOICE OF NON-FICTION

**The Time of My Life**  Denis Healey

'Denis Healey's memoirs have been rightly hailed for their intelligence, wit and charm ... *The Time of My Life* should be read, certainly for pleasure, but also for profit ... he bestrides the post-war world, a Colossus of a kind' – *Independent.* 'No finer autobiography has been written by a British politician this century' – *Economist*

**Chasing the Monsoon**  Alexander Frater

'Frater's unclouded sight unfurls the magic behind the mystery tour beautifully ... his spirited, eccentric, vastly diverting book will endure the ceaseless patter of travel books on India' – *Daily Mail*. 'This is travel writing at its best. Funny, informed, coherent and deeply sympathetic towards its subject' – *Independent on Sunday*

**Isabelle**  Annette Kobak

'A European turned Arab, a Christian turned Muslim, a woman dressed as a man; a libertine who stilled profound mystical cravings by drink, hashish and innumerable Arab lovers ... All the intricate threads of her rebellious life are to be found in Annette Kobak's scrupulously researched book' – Lesley Blanch in the *Daily Telegraph*

**Flying Dinosaurs**  Michael Johnson

Hundreds of millions of years ago, when dinosaurs walked the earth, we know that there also existed great prehistoric beasts call pterosaurs that could fly or glide. Now you can make these extraordinary creatures fly again. *Flying Dinosaurs* contain almost everything you need to construct eight colourful and thrillingly lifelike flying model pterosaurs – from the pterodactylus to the dimorphodon.

**The Italians**  Luigi Barzini

'Brilliant ... whether he is talking about the family or the Mafia, about success or the significance of gesticulation, Dr Barzini is always illuminating and amusing' – *The Times*. 'He hits his nails on the head with bitter-sweet vitality ... Dr Barzini marshals and orders his facts and personalities with the skill of an historian as well as a journalist' – *Observer*

# READ MORE IN PENGUIN

## A CHOICE OF NON-FICTION

**Riding the Iron Rooster**  Paul Theroux

Travels in old and new China with the author of *The Great Railway Bazaar*. 'Mr Theroux cannot write badly ... he is endlessly curious about places and people ... and in the course of a year there was almost no train in the whole vast Chinese rail network in which he did not travel' – Ludovic Kennedy

**Ninety-two Days**  Evelyn Waugh

In this fascinating chronicle of a South American journey, Waugh describes the isolated cattle country of Guiana, sparsely populated by an odd collection of visionaries, rogues and ranchers, and records the nightmarish experiences travelling on foot, by horse and by boat through the jungle in Brazil.

**The Life of Graham Greene**  Norman Sherry
Volume One 1904–1939

'Probably the best biography ever of a living author' – Philip French in the *Listener*. Graham Greene has always maintained a discreet distance from his reading public.This volume reconstructs his first thirty-five years to create one of the most revealing literary biographies of the decade.

**The Day Gone By**  Richard Adams

In this enchanting memoir the bestselling author of *Watership Down* tells his life story from his idyllic 1920s childhood spent in Newbury, Berkshire, through public school, Oxford and service in World War Two to his return home and his courtship of the girl he was to marry.

**A Turn in the South**  V. S. Naipaul

'A supremely interesting, even poetic glimpse of a part of America foreigners either neglect or patronize' – *Guardian*. 'An extraordinary panorama' – *Daily Telegraph*. 'A fine book by a fine man, and one to be read with great enjoyment: a book of style, sagacity and wit' – *Sunday Times*

# READ MORE IN PENGUIN

## A CHOICE OF NON-FICTION

**1001 Ways to Save the Planet**   Bernadette Vallely

There are 1001 changes that *everyone* can make in their lives today to bring about a greener environment – whether at home or at work, on holiday or away on business. Action that you can take *now*, and that you won't find too difficult to take. This practical guide shows you how.

**Bitter Fame**   Anne Stevenson

'A sobering and salutary attempt to estimate what Plath was, what she achieved and what it cost her ... This is the only portrait which answers Ted Hughes's image of the poet as Ariel, not the ethereal bright pure roving sprite, but Ariel trapped in Prospero's pine and raging to be free' – *Sunday Telegraph*

**The Complete Book of Running**   James F. Fixx

Jim Fixx's pioneering book has encouraged a sedentary generation to take to the streets. Packed with information for the beginner, the more experienced runner and the marathon winner, it explains the many benefits to be reaped from running and advises on how to overcome the difficulties. 'This book is a boon and a blessing to the multitudes who jog and run throughout the world' – Michael Parkinson

**Friends in High Places**   Jeremy Paxman

'The Establishment is alive and well ... in pursuit of this elusive, seminal circle of souls around which British institutions revolve, Jeremy Paxman ... has written a thoughtful examination, both poignant and amusing' – *Independent*

**Slow Boats to China**   Gavin Young

Gavin Young's bestselling account of his extraordinary journey in small boats through the Mediterranean, the Red Sea, the Indian Ocean and the Malaya and China Seas to China. 'A joy to read, engaging, civilised, sharply observant, richly descriptive and sometimes hilarious ... a genuine modern adventure story' – *Sunday Express*

# READ MORE IN PENGUIN

## A SELECTION OF TRUE CRIME

**The Best We Can Do**  Sybille Bedford

Her celebrated account of the trial of the Eastbourne GP John Bodkin Adams. 'A wonderfully-described account of one of the most extraordinary murder trials of the last fifty years' – Ludovic Kennedy

**The Famous Trials of Marshall Hall**  Edward Marjoribanks

Edward Marjoribanks' book, part biography, part case history, traces Sir Marshall's career and recounts his role in numerous famous cases, including the Camden Town Murder, the Brides in the Bath case and the crime passionnel at the Savoy Hotel.

**The Complete Jack the Ripper**  Donald Rumbelow

'Mr Rumbelow...sets the crimes firmly in their historical setting, examines the evidence comprehensively and scrupulously, disposes of a number of theories and legends and relates the murders to popular literature and to later similar sex crimes. He has had the advantage of access to some of Scotland Yard's most confidential papers. It is difficult to believe that any future Ripperologists will provide a fuller account'– P. D. James